This Journal Belongs To

The Starlight Poets

to
be
to bre
To tra
and get
never fe
never le
Slip awa
how

but think,

rowing time from?

ed, finite existence, do I ow to anyone

m protected piece of art.

a glass, restored, + dusted

ked, weathered like cobblestone stre

thy city of light

enetrate through

e dark spaces in my mind

art, there's a clarity of composition

at comes from a view in grey scale

But these dark spaces hide lives in the curtains of their sha

Until the sheets are pulled back

only to reveal the truth that is there—

maybe i will never know

the reason why...

but i know ill be writing postcards to heave

The Art & Poetry of Travelers

Volume Two

by R. Clift

Paris | Reims

2023

to my Starlight Poets,

Sylvie, and Kristine

This Journal

Hello there— I'm Rachel, and you've just discovered our travel journal. In the summer of 2023, I gathered a group of passionate artists to wander the enchanting streets of Paris, united by one exquisite purpose—to capture the essence of our experiences in art and poetry.

From thousands of miles away my fellow travelers arrived, drawn by the intoxicating allure of creativity and the whispers of adventure. We now call ourselves 'The Starlight Poets,' but we began as eleven strangers. It took only moments for us to feel like long-lost friends reuniting beneath the shimmering Parisian skies.

In the heart of this romantic city, something inexplicable and profoundly cosmic happens when poets gather to create and share their souls. It's as if the universe itself conspires to shower inspiration upon those who are open to its magic. Throughout our time together, we found ourselves overflowing with words, each line inspired by the beauty that enveloped us— the Seine's gentle embrace, the glow of candlelight in dim cathedrals, and the artistry of life unfolding around us.

As this was my second time hosting an Art & Poetry retreat, I entered with a heart full of hopes and dreams. I longed for my artists to discover poetry, meaning, and deep connection amidst the charm of Paris. What unfolded was nothing short of pure magic. To this day, it's a challenge to express what this journey—and these remarkable poets—mean to me and to one another.

Emma, Freydis, J.S., Kassidy, Kendall, Leisly, Mary-Anne, Sunshine, Vanessa, Laura— thank you for being my guiding stars. Thank you for weaving your art and poetry into this anthology. May the world be as entranced by your words as I am by each and every one of you.

May we, always, shine through the dark.

Ever yours,

xx R.

Itinerary

Day One - July 9th:
- Arrive in Paris
- First dinner together
- Wander under the stars

Day Two - July 10th:
- Street Art Tour in Montmartre
- Art & Poetry Workshop One
- Get lost in The Louvre Museum
- Write poetry beneath the Eiffel Tower

Day Three - July 11th:
- Tour of Le Marais district
- Walk to Notre Dame & Shakespeare and Co.
- Art & Poetry Workshop Two
- Watch the Eiffel Tower sparkle

Day Four - July 12th:
- Travel to Versailles & explore
- Dance in the gardens
- Visit Marie Antoinette's Estate & Hamlet
- Write Exquisite Corpse Poetry together

Day Five - July 13th:
- Travel to the Champagne region
- Tour Vranken Pommery Cellars
- Explore underground art gallery
- Visit Saint-Remy Museum & Reims Cathedral
- Art & Poetry Workshop Three
- Travel back to Paris
- Goodbye dinner & roam under city lights

Day Six - July 14th:
- Stroll by the Seine
- Final goodbyes & fly home

Traveler

Table of Contents

Le Chemin de la Mémoire

The Travelers
as captured by L.A. Clift

I spent a week with nine dreamers, poets who turned to me with leather bound pages, their eyes full of stars and city lights and saying-

"I've spilled my ink- will you tell me what you see?"

- L.A. Clift

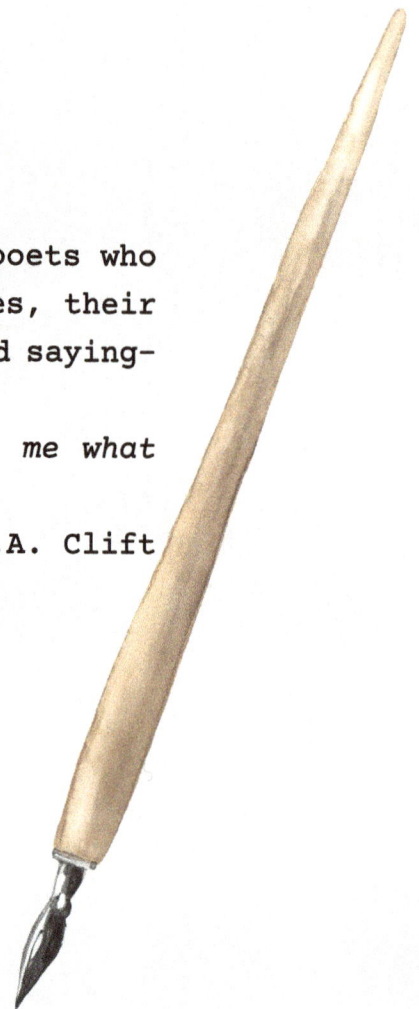

Here, I would like to formally introduce our travelers, dreamers, & artists. Laura wrote poems about them as if she were introducing characters in an enchanting novel set in Paris.
- R.

Tour Guide
Sylvie

She is a page of a history book caught on the winds of Paris. Flying fast- and in any possible direction, she guides you over cobble stones, through alleys and gardens and palaces, all while sharing the stories of the past. And yet- there is still more to discover. She is the chaos and the mind and the heart of Paris.

Emma

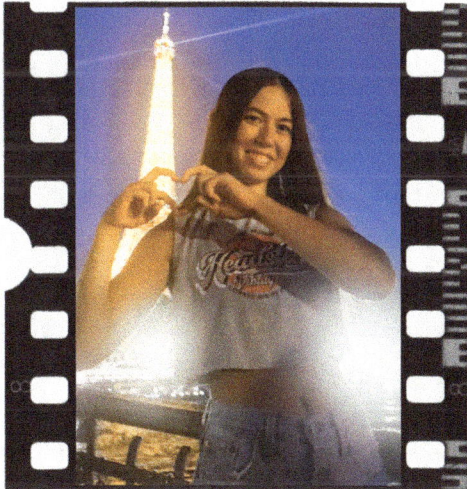

She is both young and ancient- the playful river rushing through the city. Along the banks she laughs, captures reflections, holds secrets whispered from bridges for centuries. Always somewhere between where she has been and where she will go. Endless possibilities are at her fingertips and she runs, no- flies to meet them- as naturally as the Siene flows to sea.

Freydis

She is the stardust that falls from the sky each night to fill the lanterns of Paris. Carefully, she takes apart every bright memory and strings them into pages of poems. There is magic within her words and moonlight caught in her eyes. If you have the chance- take her hand and dance through the endless starry skies as she crafts her world with drying ink.

J.S.

He is the quietness to be found in the bustling City of Light. The instant of silence in a garden, the cool shadows of a cathedral hall, the birds resting above on windowsills. A poem read quietly to friends by the Siene. Even in a place so loud and overwhelming- there is peace to be found by his side.

Kassidy

"I'm not really a poet," she tells me- and I see her stop to watch the leaves rustle above in the sunlight. She leaps to the ground and runs- just to capture a memory to hold in her hand. A cat in a window is enough to bring a smile to her face. She can see the stories within the museums, behind the glass. "I'm not really a poet," she tells me- and I wonder when she'll realize she always has been.

Kendall

Her heart is crafted of ink and paper. With eager joy she reaches for Paris and finds a wealth of art and knowledge in return. They are friends, I think- the poet, her books, and the city of lights. Just as she longs to learn every story, witness every work of art- Paris longs to hear her words.

Leisly

Poetry sparkles from her like midnight on the Siene. She is the laughter in the cafes, the bubbles in champagne, the music filtering from somewhere around the corner or from another life. "There is still wonder to be found," she tells me. And with a silver pen she writes- her poems a whirlwind of joy to lift us towards the horizon with a whole world to explore and no time to waste.

Mary-Anne

She is as timeless as the city itself. A muse escaped from the Louvre and is walking among us- taking her time getting to know the world again. Beauty and history catch her eye around each bend in the road. Her hands reach for her pen and journal and even when her mind screams "it's been too long" she takes to the pages and writes the clouds away. Her poetry is timeless.

Sunshine

Paris called to her. This city of forgotten history and old dreams and new discovery. She carries the depths of night- but still, there is light to be found. Around every corner- something to capture. To remember. To feel. To love. I think the city calls to those who have been shattered like glass- and yet still find a way to let light shine out, to go on creating, to go on loving.

Vanessa

She is the breath of the open sea breezing in to the bustling city. She is street art running through Paris, leaving memories behind, painting walls with poetry- only here for an instant. Made of dreams and dust from very far away, she leaves a lock on a bridge and is as much part of the city as any tower or half-smiling painting. She is the breath of the open sea leaving Paris a little warmer and brighter than she found it.

Trip Host

Rachel

How do you pin down a constellation? She is made of many stars. Blinding and faint. Many words. Familiar darkness and pinpoints of hope carefully strung into intricate webs of mystery and truth for the passing stargazer. But you'll only glimpse the brightest. For those willing to brave the longest nights, she'll carefully drop the dimmest starlight into your palm, hoping to the moon you will catch it. Soft as a prayer. A promise. If you do, if you stay- you may be able to finally know her as she is, in the space between the stars.

Starlight

By the light of the sun,
Do not let me forget,
Those souls I've grown to love.
Starlight, star bright,
Those poets who shined brighter
than the moon at night.
Each of us like stars in the sky,
Arranged in this moment in time.
We became a new constellation,
One that Orion would envy.
And it's no coincidence,
It's fate, call it destiny.
We are burning and fading,
In this iridescent galaxy.
We will soon travel new paths.
Become lost in our own worlds.
Discover a new universe,
Remembering the stars we once called home.

- Mary-Anne

La Dame de Fer

Poets gather in the grass to capture
some sort of beauty-
the sun sinks below the horizon,
illuminating their inspiration
as a spotlight would shine
upon a star actress on stage.
They all gaze in awe
of her magnificence, wondering
what it must be like to be so adored.
Hoping- one day-
to feel just as significant.

- R. Clift

Sketch by Emma

Exploring the Tuileries
Garden & writing beneath
the Eiffel Tower

by Vanessa

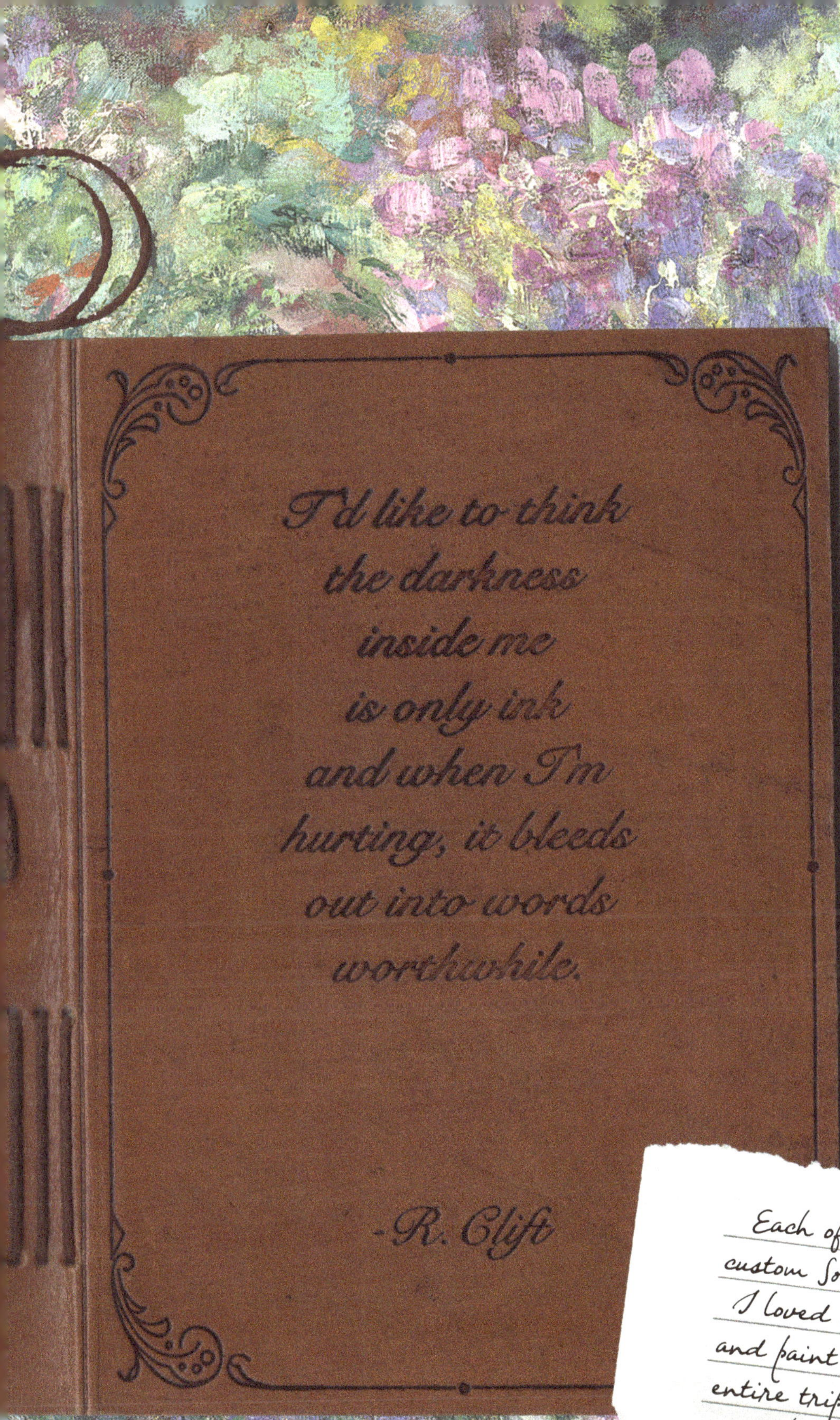

I'd like to think
the darkness
inside me
is only ink
and when I'm
hurting, it bleeds
out into words
worthwhile.

-R. Clift

Each of my travelers recieved a
custom Soothi leather journal!
I loved seeing them write, sketch,
and paint in them throughout the
entire trip. Every artist deserves a &
beutiful journal to fill.

I taught our first Art & Poetry workshop in a garden beside Sacré-Cœur within the Montmartre district of Paris. It was an absolute dream to teach here!

Art & Poetry Workshop 1

Topics:
— Ekphrasis Poetry
— Perspective & Point of View
— "Beauty Exists So Close to Agony"

Ekphrasis (Etymology) {Pronounced Ek-fruh-sis}
- ek: "out of"
- phrasis: "speech or expression"
Ekphrastic Poetry is a poem inspired by a work of art.
A vivid description of a work of art, simply put— it
is a conversation between poetry and art. The poet
interprets the art and then creates a narrative that
represents his or her reaction to it.

> Ekphrasis Poem 1: While on our street art
> tour, pay attention to the contemporary graffiti
> and the Salvador Dali Gallery— write an
> Ekphrastic poem with one of these pieces.
>
> Ekphrasis Poem 2: Now in The Louvre, write
> another Ekphrasis poem with an ancient or
> classic piece of art. Which one calls to you?
> Will you answer?
> —Consider your point of view & perspective.

Emma

E.R.

Kindred Spirits

Tell me a story?
Il était une fois or *Once upon a time*
However you tell it,
do not tell me of fairies or castles
though they still shine in my eyes.
What captivates my little soul nowadays
Are kindred spirits and happenstance.
This way of growing up
I can accept.
Lingering conversations in coffee shops
and pausing near the door
Leave your fingerprints on my skin
a hug, a kiss goodbye
And your imprint on my soul
A wave, a glance in parting
Before you're gone in the blink of an eye.

EMMA RIDDOCH

Why I Hate Museums

I think art was meant

To be

Enjoyed as it was made

Apart from others

From the soul

Up close

And from a distance

With considerance

Of the emotion and story

Inside you

EMMA RIDDOCH

E.R.

There are so many people

That throughout my life have lit up

And added wholeheartedly to the landscape of my soul.

They leave so quickly, just as they had come,

And as soon as the moment passes,

and the traces of their presence

Remain only in my soul,

Our shared memories come to a halt,

And begin to fade

And every time, I mourn the loss of them,

Though these special people and I have

Never been so close

But they brightened my world anyway.

Soon, I'll forget all of the things that

Endeared me to you

But I'll never forget the twinkle

In your eye

And the sparkle of your glimmering soul

That knows me no longer

To Sylvie

EMMA RIDDOCH

These pages are soft
They hold my fears so gently,
The leather is so supple
In my tears I grasp it firmly
Misery is the best company
For those who suffer alone
Sauf un ami
Qui n'attends pas en retour

overstimulation; peace

speak not here; it is too loud
let us go; into the quiet recesses
hold my hand; and this crowd will not separate us
whisper in my ear; i hope it's not important
i listen only to your breath; and my pounding heartbeat
heat is stifling; now it hugs
us both; now free
flared senses; quiet their roar
the absence of need; is the space where love makes its home
and my most pressing need; has faded
with you; all to my own

EMMA RIDDOCH

La rage feminine

This city was birthed from feminine rage
It's the way the revolution started,
With the woman being the sign,
Flooding the streets because they can't feed their children
It's in the muse, sexualized and perverted
But still the source of all inspiration
Divine energy is always distorted
through the lens of translation anyway
It's in the way women have taken
men's fashion for their own over the centuries in
The form of heels, suits, jeans,
And fashion runs this city
La Seine has washed (like women have)
every drop of spilt blood pouring from hundred year wars
from her banks
Like a bloody cycle
But women know that one too
The brick and mortar of the patriarchy is the sacrifice of women
And Paris herself is itching for justice.

EMMA RIDDOCH

BASTILLE, 2023
EMMA RIDDOCH

E.R.

There is such beauty in enjoying life

Because we are monuments to our souls

When you are your greatest

Investment and muse

That power comes through you from beyond

And pulls at the world around you,

Like a child's stick

Dragging through the web of life.

The accoutrements of this woman's monument,

Were Barbie curls and a sundress;

A beer and the river;

A man waiting for her downstream;

And she captivated us all

More than any painting or sculpture

She held the moment

And us our breaths

Before she walked away.

EMMA RIDDOCH

23

Visiting the Cathédrale Notre-Dame & Shakespeare and Company Bookstore

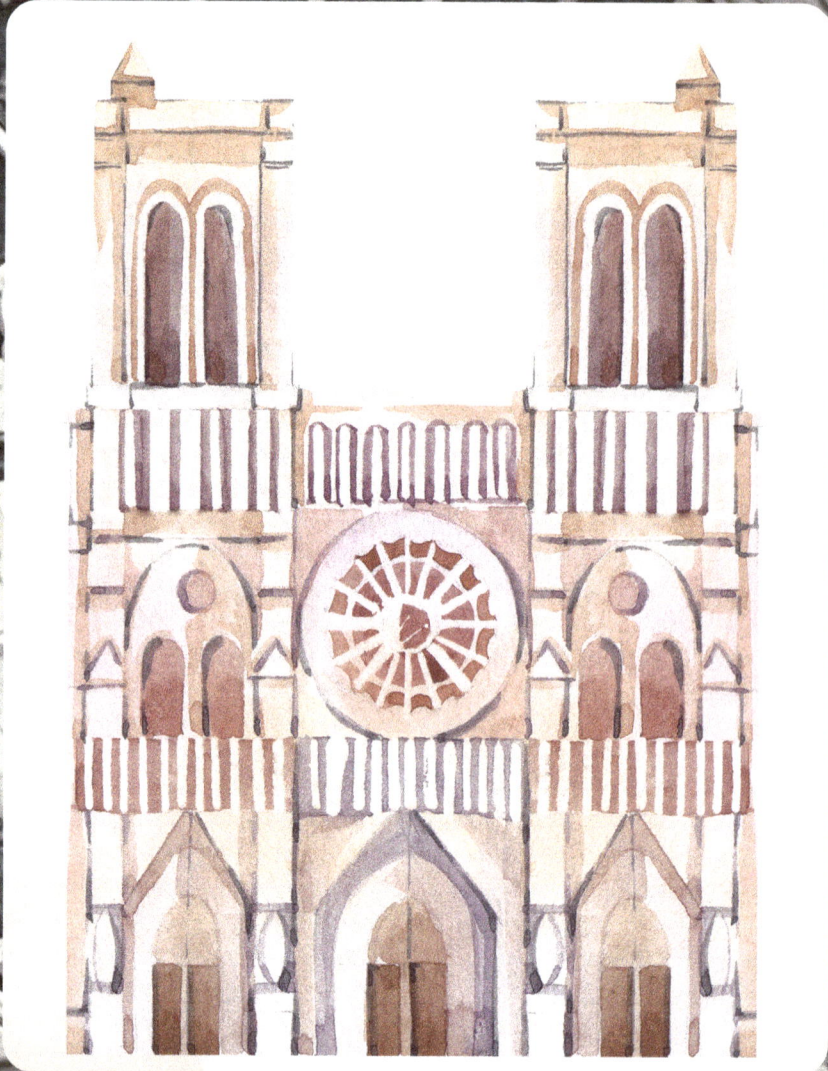

Les Échos du Passé

For eight centuries I have endured,
your lady of seven sorrows-
my stone grotesques have gazed
down at you night and day-
reminding you of your own
mortality- my heart, a
rose window- shining despite
the damage it has withstood.
My spired fingers reaching
towards heaven may
have been burned but
do not be fooled- I will
reach again,
I will feel the hands of god
through the laborers who
restore me-
just as when they built these walls
for the first time so long ago.
    Tell all those
    who behold me-
not even the fires of hell itself
can extinguish my holiness.

- R. Clift

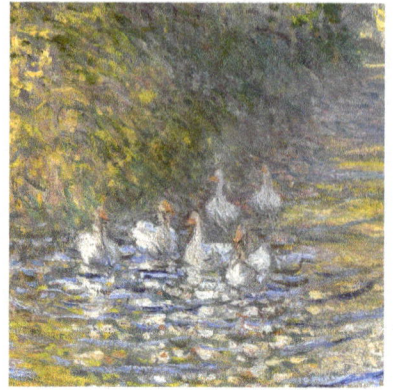

Freydis

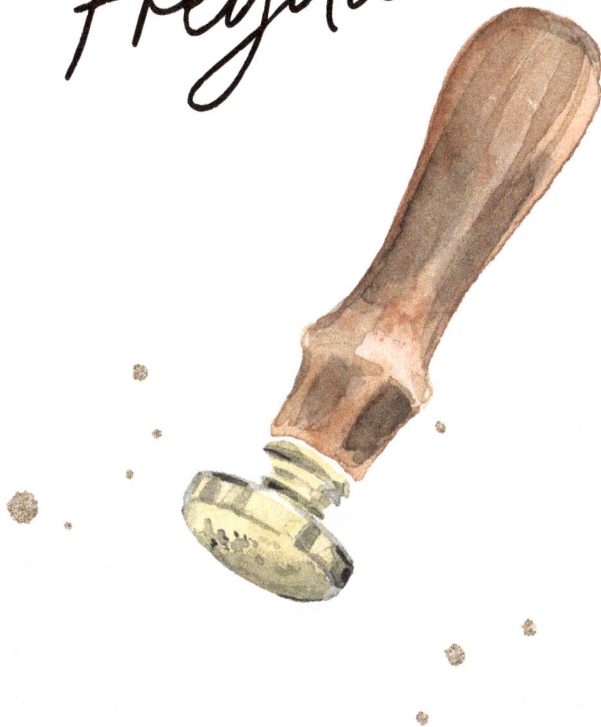

Somewhere in Paris,
a candle is lit in someone's memory.

Somewhere in Paris,
someone is praying for love.

Somewhere in Paris,
church bells echo through empty alleyways.

Somewhere in Paris,
I leave our forever in a graveyard.

Blue velvet rises,
pulled to the sides and
beyond the fading chandelier.
I steady my breathing,
gingerly twisting the ends of my shawl
instead of laying patiently in my lap.

Moments ago, I was half blind,
looking for a contact lens
at the bottom of a bag in a hotel bathroom.
Now I'm here with you,
and we're here with them.

They stand among the echoes and ghosts
in the heaviest silence the byzantine night
can stand. But there's more to it- to them.
Surrounding their stage is a spectacle of
viridian and gold, shrouded in pearl luster.

You reach for my hand, but pull back
as the orchestra begins to play.

The curtain finishes its ascension.
The shadows stay still as they're illuminated.

This isn't an opera.
This is life.

The show begins.

FREYDIS LOVA

Pink lips taste the sweetest
when they're feeding you lies.

She says, *Je vous aime.*

Her lips stain his red.

He asks me with his eyes.

It shouldn't catch me off guard—

he's always been a gentleman—

but for some reason, it does.

Maybe because I wasn't expecting it.

His eyes are a language

I speak but once a year,

yet will always understand

as clearly as my mother tongue.

I hand him the silver chain

and pull my hair out of the way

as he positions himself behind me.

He's kind enough to be careful

not to brush his fingers against my neck.

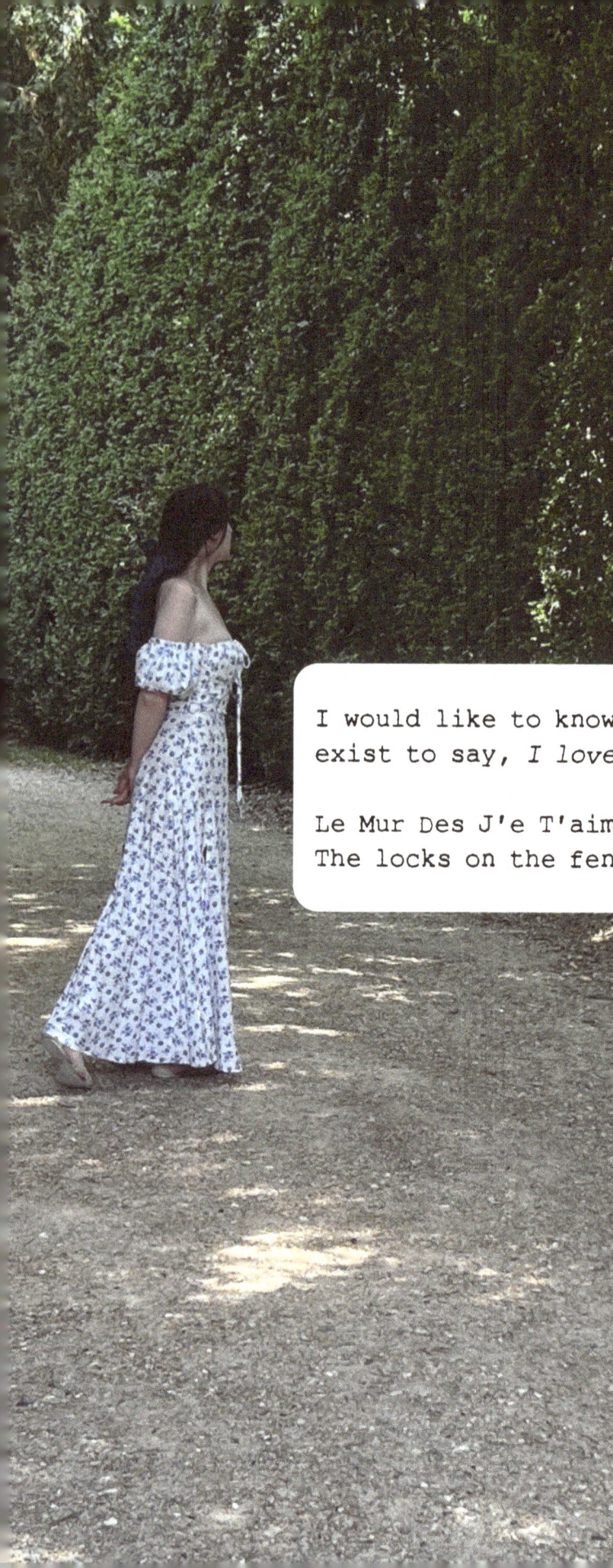

I would like to know how many ways
exist to say, *I love you.*

Le Mur Des J'e T'aime says, *311.*
The locks on the fences say, *endless.*

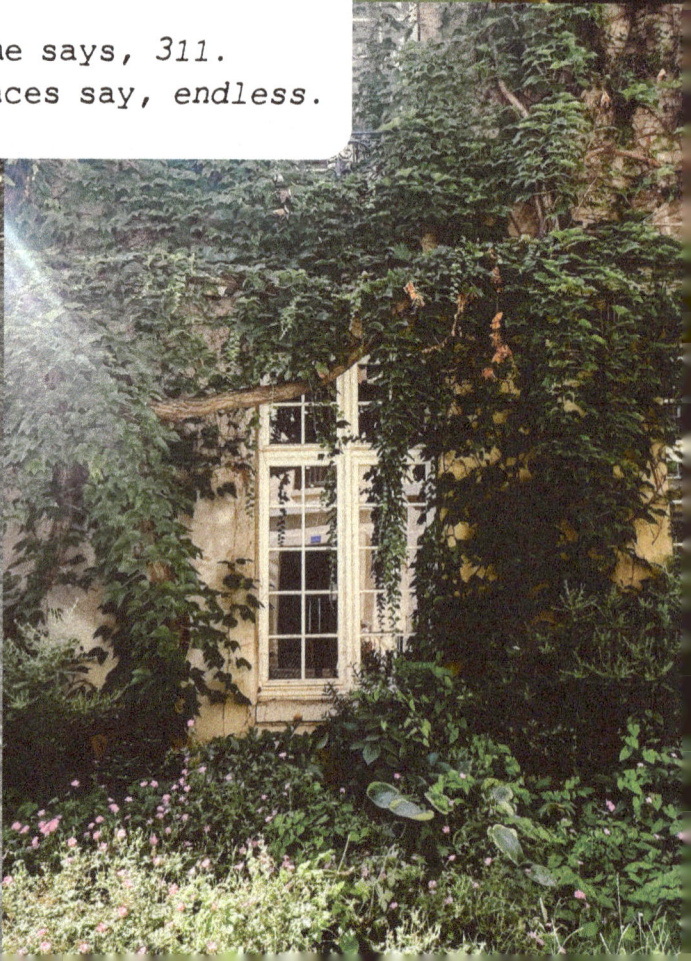

How many times can a poet write *I*?
How many times can we selfishly center
our words around ourselves?
How many times can we string you along
through our lives, our happiness, our pain?

Poets love pain best.
He's our closest friend.
We hug shadows and bloom in cemetery orchards,
watered with the tears we shed for others,
for those who don't know the end yet.

Our ends so very often meet us in the middle of the story.
So how many times?
I want to know the answer.

But right now, I want to know you more.

Every road, every river, every piece of art
that embellishes your streets.
I want to meet you on a bridge
and see how we begin—
this new, temporary life.

I want to know why Vincent and Claude loved you so—
if I can love you just as much.

Please, don't let us be strangers anymore.

We're nearly there.
The quietness of this place
suddenly breaks.

He's the old man of Montmarte,
sitting on the corner with an accordion.

La Vie en Rose.

I find a euro in my wallet
and drop it in his cup.

The cat atop the instrument lifts his head
as if to thank me.
I take out another euro.

I can't thank one and not the other.

....

I stand there for a few more songs.
The cat sways his tail and tilts his head,
content with nestling down on the other end
of the accordion. His purrs are barely audible
above the hum of keys, keeping time.
He closes his eyes and smiles,
ears tilted back. His owner smiles down at him.

I think he plays more for the cat than the people.

MONTMARTE, 2023
FREYDIS LOVA

Somewhere between the deep green and gold,
I see them- my familiar faces.
There's thirteen of them, laying imperfectly
in acrylic in front of ivory, pale blue,
and every other color
of a muted, Florence sky.

I know these flowers are meant to be French,
but even still, I can't help but think
that somehow, the artist and I have
a thread connecting our histories-

all of our sunflowers.

FREYDIS LOVA

FREYDIS.LOVA

My dear, darling one,

I recognize that look in your eyes.

An endless darkness has been broken

by breath and embrace.

He is haloed in all things light-

this savior of yours, so tenderly

leaning over you as if to shield you

from all things wicked except himself.

To shield you from us.

But you don't notice us.

You only see him.

And as you reach up to pull him back down

into another kiss, my heart breaks

because everyone knows your fate but you.

An ekphrasis poem capturing
"Psyche Revived by Cupid's Kiss"
by Antonio Canova

FREYDIS LOVA

"Death of Ophelia"
Eugène Delacroix

You had her entire life to immortalize,
and yet you chose her death.
Chose the moment she fell,
the moment she crumbled
beneath the brink. That's your way,
though, isn't it, Eugène?
To see a woman's weakness
as a beautiful tragedy
instead of accepting their strength?
You make the river rise,
the waves appear far taller than
they really are. You kiss us
until we can't breathe,
and laugh as we gasp for air.
You could have chosen any moment
of happiness. Instead, you have made it
so history will always know how she left us
without telling us whose fault it was.
They will see her as beautiful but crazy.
The women will stand silently
and send a prayer back in time
in hopes that somewhere, somehow,
the pages will change to tell the story
of a woman who left without leaving the earth.

FREYDIS. LOVA

The old man closes his book,
sighs, and looks back at the angels.
As the pages fall forward,
I can see that they're all filled
with the same sad face and wings.
With her hands over her heart,
she watches him leave again and again.
She can't go with him.

He fiddles with his wedding band.
Centuries before he was even a thought,
someone sculpted his wife
so that even when Fate tore them apart,
they could still somehow be together.

My lover tastes like watered-down wine
and cigarettes. Or maybe just the wine,
and the cigarettes are from the midnight air,
ash falling in front of twinkling lights.
Except we aren't standing in front of the tower,
and it's seven in the morning.

So why doesn't he taste like coffee and pain au chocolate?

I kiss him again, hoping to find the answer.

This place is a church itself-
statues formed of sonnets,
saints and sinners alike, gathered
to pay tithes and offerings.
We read from the same scriptures,
sing praise of our saviors,
share books with strangers.
Leather-bound and paperback press
together in windows- stained glass
our Sun can't shine through.

This is the place where poets come to worship.

My Dear Dante,

It seems as though you've found me again.

Hell was supposed to be a burning inferno of flame,

but it's freezing.

My fingers are speckled with blue and white,

numbing with every step we descend.

Footsteps fall over the record—

music, a memory, and fading fast.

We chose this path.

A group of happy sinners getting tipsy on champagne.

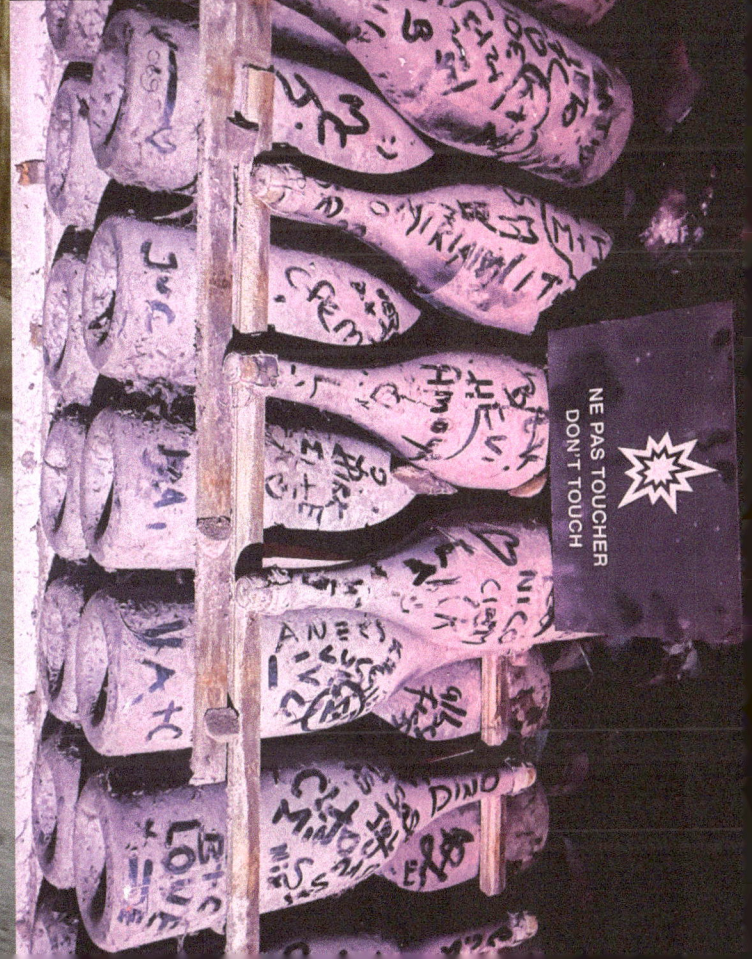

NE PAS TOUCHER
DON'T TOUCH

The tears of the forgotten
meet their end in a room of echos
and decay. A desk sits in the center,
snow and salt eating away
at its legs and body.
Still, it stands with what little strength
it has left. The snow falls. The ice creeps.
The pens dry up and the papers burn.
My Dear Dante,
is this the poets' circle?

FREYDIS LOVA

Exploring the streets of Paris with a group of bright-eyed poets felt like a long-awaited

dream come true.

Change yourself to change the world

Che tutto arda di Amore e Poesia

l'Amour
est clair comme le jour,
l'Amour
est simple comme le bonjour,
l'Amour
est nu comme la main,
c'est ton Amour et le mien.

Jacques
Prévert

We went on a Street Art Tour through Montmartre & visited the "Wall of Love"

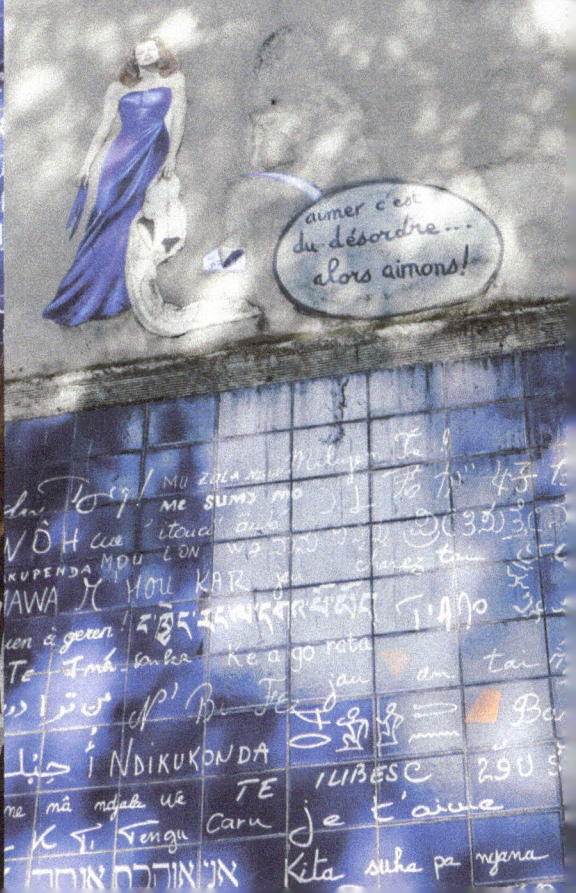

aimer c'est du désordre... alors aimons!

Details of Paris— elegant cathedrals, the resilience of nature, and tiny friends...

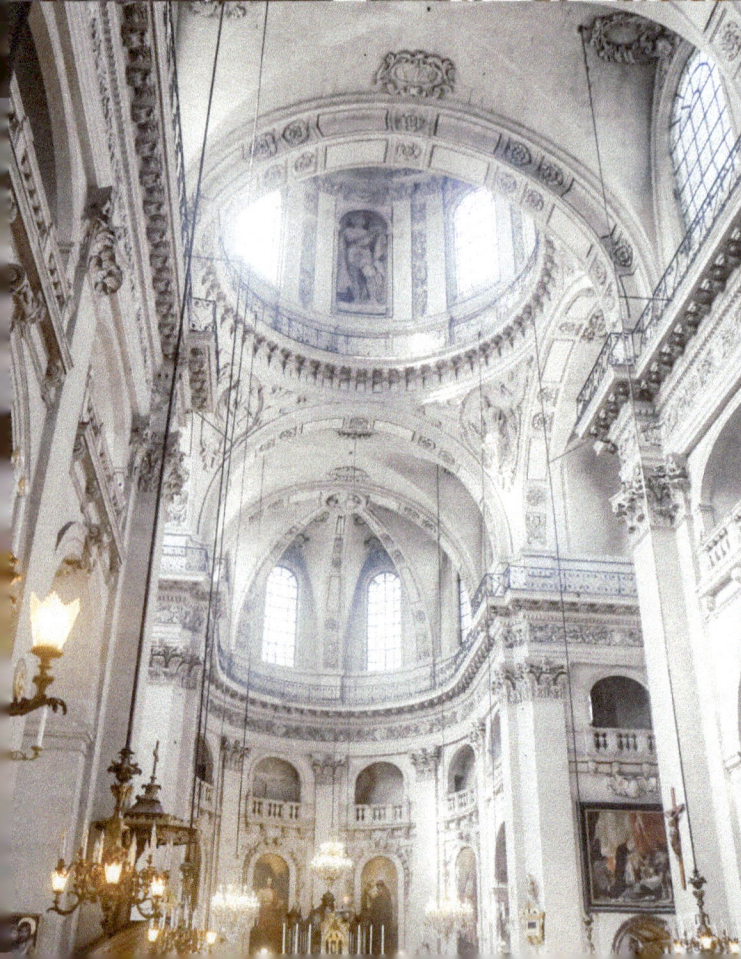

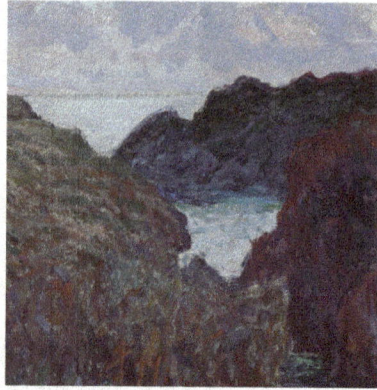

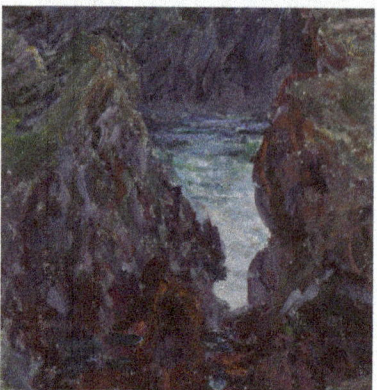

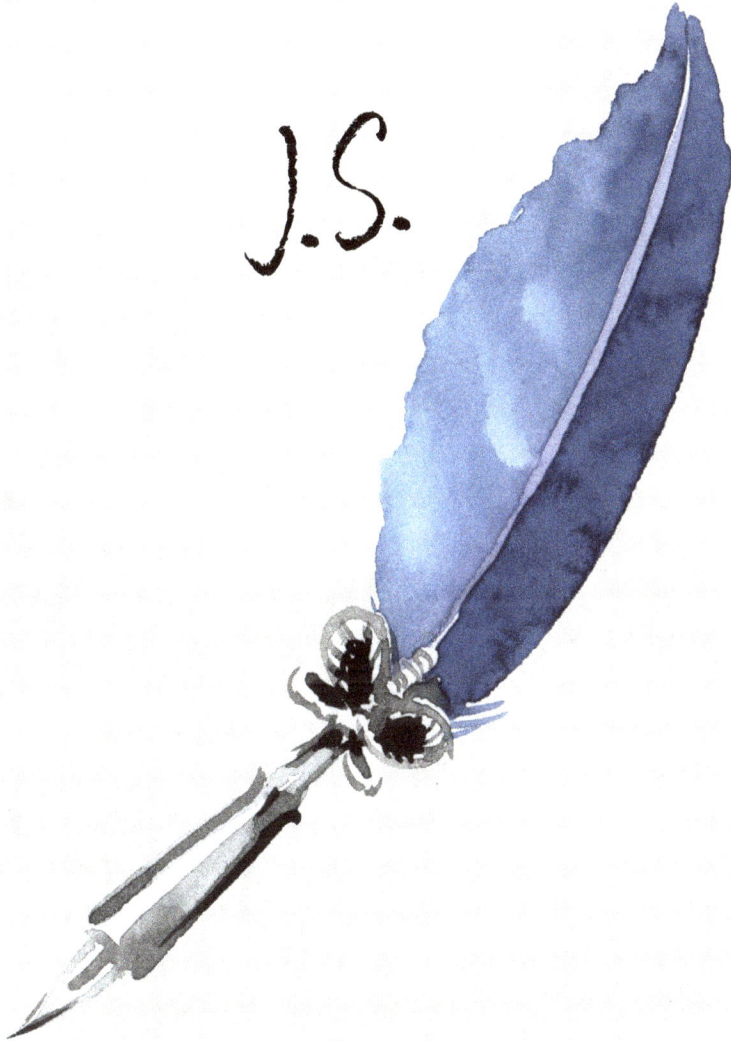

I wish there wasn't such beauty

in the wounds

you left me with

For in the face of which--

what voice is there

to give my pain

It is such a subtle suffering

that burns bright as the sun

yet just as silent

How so to am I,

with a warmth for all the world to feel

and none to know

how I am being burnt alive

by beauty

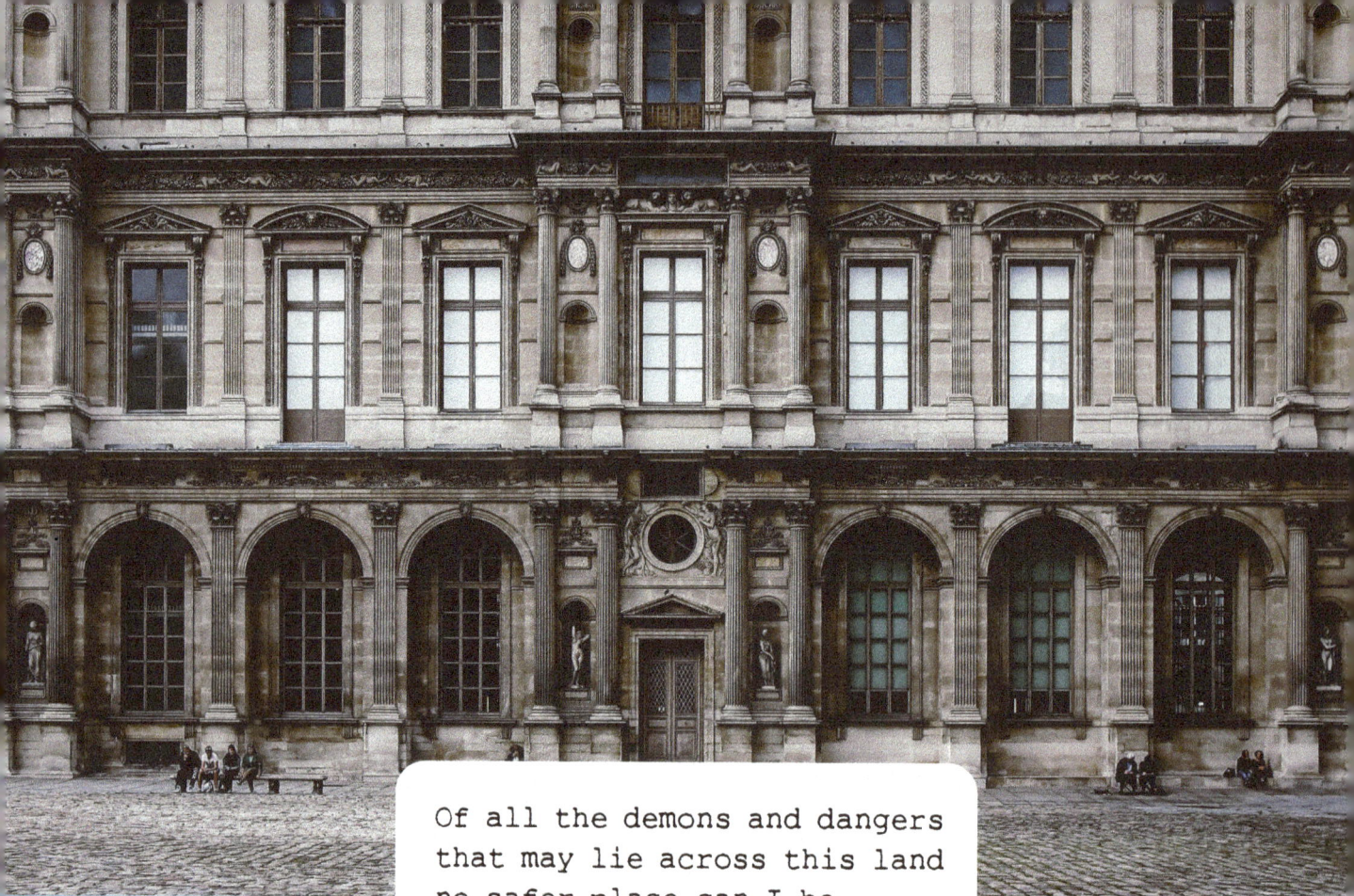

Of all the demons and dangers
that may lie across this land
no safer place can I be
than in the corner of a cafe
with but a book to protect me
                        - J.S.

Save your love

for that

which is yet

to come

Rather than

wasting it

on what once

was

The Louvre Museum is endless—
I wish we could have had days
and days to spend here!

Writing ekphrasis poems—
my favorite pastime in museums...

Whose Sculptor is Unknown

You were made to be free, yet
they've trapped you, haven't they?
You tried so often to
claw your way out-
they took away your ability
to reach for the door.
I see you searching over
the heads of onlookers-
some awestruck- most
irreverent and aggressive-
as you search for a way out,
a chance to escape.
But they've sentenced you
to a pedastal and roped
you off- destined to
be gawked at by strangers
who will never even
know your name.

Venus de Milo
120BC

- R. Clift

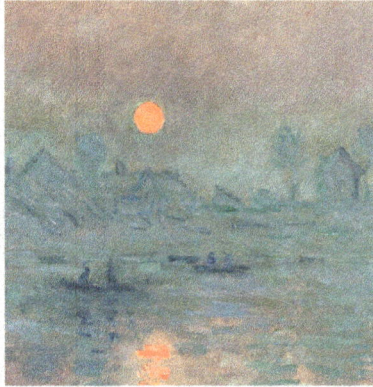

Kassidy

She walks and runs through the streets of Paris

not letting anyone or anything get in her way.

Only stopping for food and a bit of shade every now and then!

She is an open book full of knowledge and history lessons

who never fights the urge to share

and teach.

She says... Preach!

With her maternal instincts showing she guides her students

through the city and beyond while

making sure they are gathering each and every

piece of the puzzle along the way.

She wears her heart on her sleeve for all to see,

She is as happy as can be,

She is Sylvie!

KASSIDY FISK

Same same

Everyone's the same.

People here,

People there,

People everywhere.

Following one another,

not giving any extra space.

Trying to breathe, take it all in,

and capture each moment

of the past that once was the present.

The beautiful pieces of history

that only exist here,

and are protected by the walls

so strongly crafted together.

The Louvre

A historical sight

you only dream about visiting

It is here,

It is waiting,

It is beautiful.

KASSIDY FISK

There she is in all her beauty,

standing tall and full of fury!

People stay and wait for hours,

she only sparkles a few times a night.

Strike that pose!

Take that photo!

Okay let's go—

the moments over.

Watch her sparkle!

THIS IS YOUR
LITTLE
REMINDER
THAT YOU
ARE LOVED.

THIS IS YOUR
LITTLE
REMINDER
THAT YOU
ARE LOVED

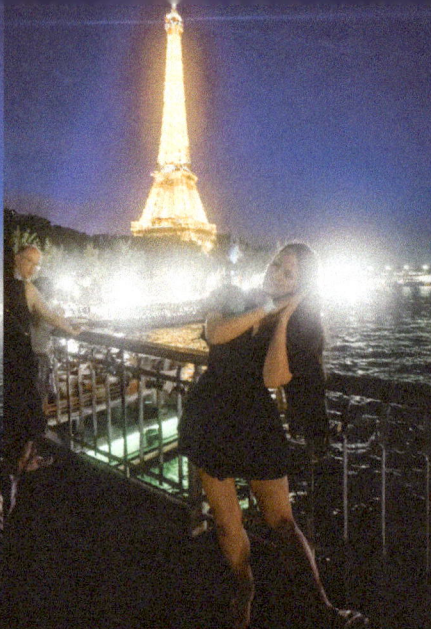

We found the best place to watch the Eiffel Tower sparkle & had an impromptu photoshoot!

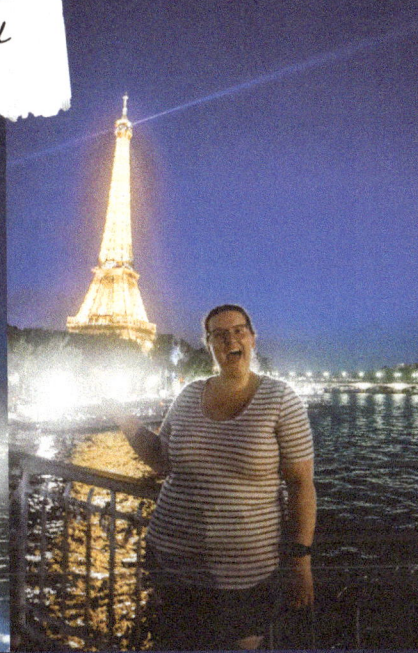

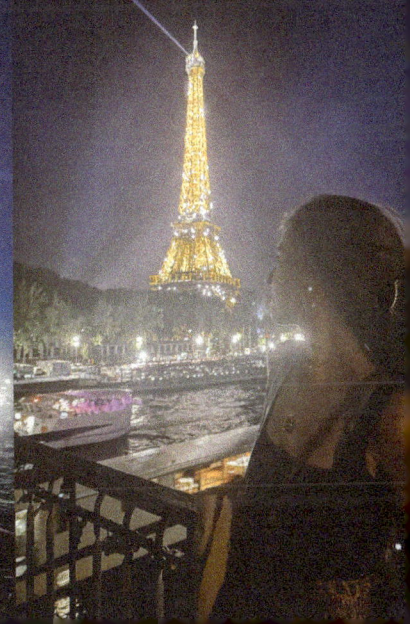

I taught our second Art & Poetry
workshop beneath the Eiffel Tower—
right next to the Seine. Many of my
poets read their writing aloud here.
I'm infinitely proud of them.

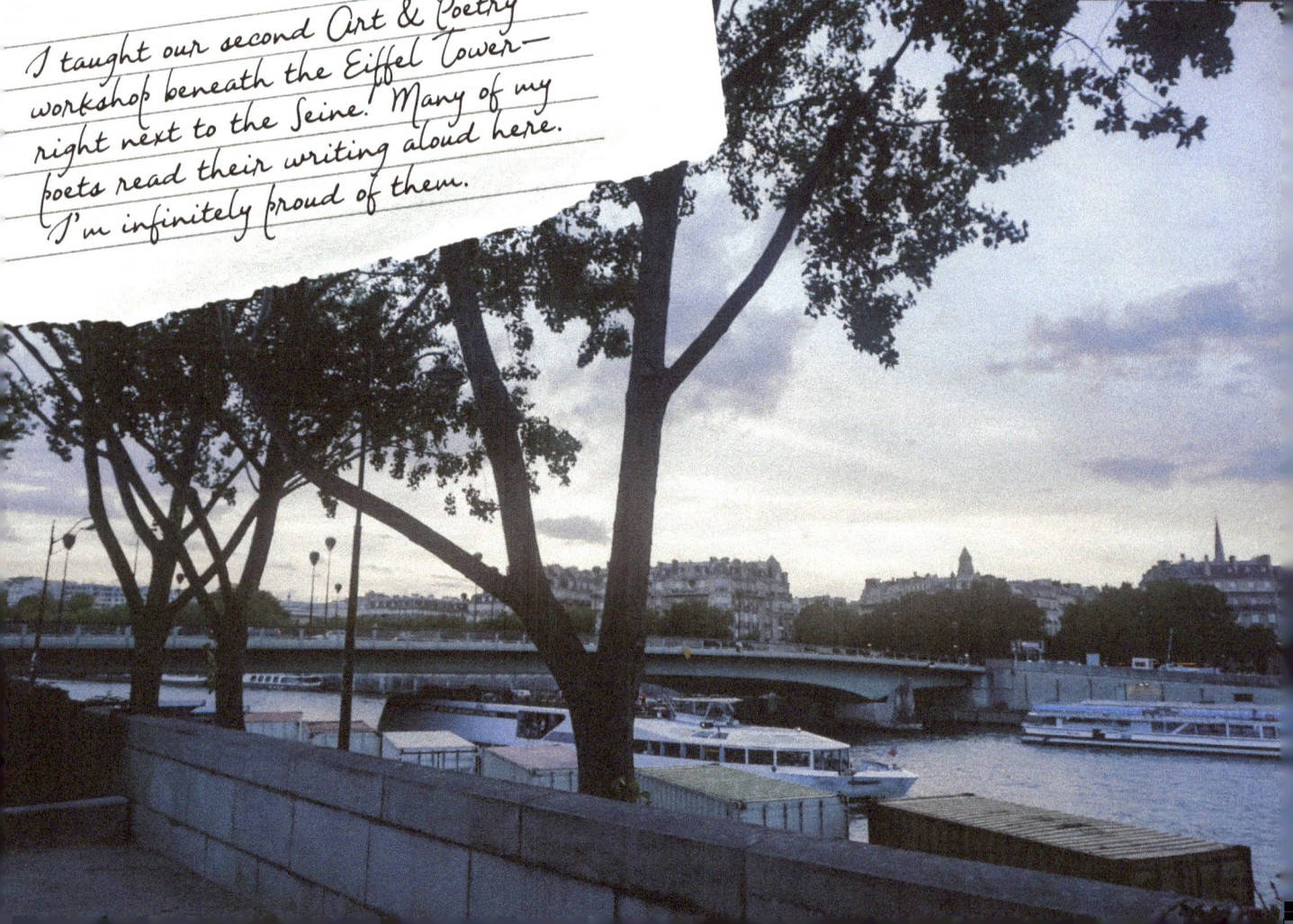

Art & Poetry Workshop 2

Topics:
— Poetry as a Memory Keeper
— Experiential Poetry — Ordinary as Extraordinary
— Exquisite Corpse — Small Group Poems

"Exquisite Corpse is a collaborative poetry game that traces its roots to the Parisian Surrealist movement. Exquisite Corpse is played by several people, each of whom writes 3 verses on a sheet of paper, folds the paper to conceal all but the last line, and passes it on to the next poet for their contribution. This is a great way to collaborate with other poets, and to free oneself from imaginative constraints or habits."

Prompt 1: Soon these moments will be only memories, and some details will fade. Immortalize a moment in a single poem— so ten years from now you may remember.

Prompt 2: Write an experiential poem about a seemingly ordinary happenstance from today. Use vivid imagery and specific detail to take the reader on a journey, as if they were standing right beside you.

Exquisite Corpse I

Heart shaped leaves dangle in the City of Love-
some are as split and cracked as own.
My heart dangles just as precariously,

as fragile as the crystals that reflect the light.
The sun shines in to cast brightness & shadows
with your reflections on the mirror-

I try and soak in
each fleeting moment
for we are living on borrowed time,

but I can't help but think,
who we are borrowing time from?
What of this varied, finite existence, do I owe to anyone...

I am not some protected piece of art-
kept behind a glass, restored, & dusted.
I am cracked , weathered like cobblestone streets-

I beg this City of Light
to penetrate through
these dark spaces in my mind.

In art, there's a clarity of composition
that comes from a view in grey scale-
but these dark spaces hide things in the curtains of their shadows,

until the sheets are pulled back
only to reveal the truth that is there-

maybe I will never know
     the reason why...
but I know I'll be writing postcards to heaven, forever.

— Emma, Vanessa, & Sunshine

Heart shaped leaves dangle in the city of Love   ER

Some are a split and cracked as my 'own

My heart dangles just as precariously,

As fragile as the crystals that reflect the light.   MW

The sun shines in to cast brightness + shadows

with your reflections on the mirror

i try and soak in   ST

each fleeting moment,

for we are living on ~~borrowed~~ time

But I can't help but think,   ER

who we are borrowing time from?

What of this varied, finite existence, do I owe to anyone...

I am not some protected piece of art,

kept behind a glass, restored, + dusted.   MW

I am cracked, weathered like cobblestone streets

i beg this city of light   ST

to penetrate through

these dark spaces in my mind

In art, there's a clarity of composition   ER

that comes from a view in grey scale

But these dark spaces hide in the curtains of their shadows

Until the sheets are pulled back   MW

only to reveal the truth that is there —

maybe i will never know   ST

the reason why...

but i ~~know~~ ill be writing postcards to heaven, forever

Emma Hiddleston
Vanessa Wilson
Sunshine Alexandria

07.12.23

He loves me, he loves me not.
I count petals as fate decides my future,
my heart already knowing the answer.

Though now I find myself with even more questions

I wonder what would become of me should I finally

find that which I'm looking for, who will I be then?

or rather, who will I be, for that time, then,

for are we not constantly changing? L.A.

tearing molds, ripping seams, spilling into the world countless times, differently

Am I too torn to mend?

How can someone such as myself be stitched back together?

A too-full heart beats an empty rhythm in a hollow chamber.

Yet there are none that know the strength it takes

to bear such a burden   none that hear my screams of silence

That strength which defeat my darkness demons
   gentle

Demons that cannot be satiated
by means of avoidance, vengeance or spite —
it takes a labor of love, and an unending toll, on your soul, to rise beyond

But rise I must, above the ocean and her stars,
reflected in blue and grey and green, all too familiar.

I fear that, even though you're not here, I'm still drowning in your eyes.

Your eyes that sparkled so much so that put all of the
                                              which
stars of night to shame

For how could they compare to you, you who was made of magic

Though not the kind made of potions of spells
I speak of magic found solely in the mundane
I speak of magic too extraordinary to explain
                                              — Heartless Nomad

Exquisite Corpse II

He loves me, he loves me not.
I count the petals as fate decides my future,
my heart already knowing th answer

though now I find myself with even more questions.
I wonder what would become of me should I finally
find that which I'm looking for, who will I be then?

Or rather, who will I be, for that time, then,
for are we not constantly changing?
Tearing molds, ripping seams, spilling into the world
countless times, differently...

Am I too torn to mend?
How can someone such as myself be stitched back together?
A too-full heart beats an empty rhythm in a hollow chamber,

yet there are none that know the strength it takes
to bear such a burden- none that hear my screams of silence-
that gentle strength which defeat my dark demons.

Demons that cannot be satiated
by means of avoidance, vengance or spite-
it takes a labor of love and an unending toll on your soul,
to rise beyond-

but rise I must, above the ocean and her stars,
reflected in blue and grey and green, all too familiar.
I fear that, even though you're not here, I'm still drowning in
your eyes.

Your eyes which sparkled so much that they put all
the stars to shame-
For how could they compare to you, you who was made of magic-

though not the kind made of potions, of spells,
I speak of magic found solely in the mundane-
I speak of magic too extraordinary to explain.

- Freydis, J.S., & Leisly

Exquisite Corpse III

You stand in a garden of endless beauty,
your bold stance tells me you belong here.
Your smile tells me you know a secret

and through these paintings I can hear your story-
these rooms so full of life and laughter-
with so much history between these walls,

I carry the weight on my shoulders,
thinking of all possibilities that could happen at any time-
like a star exploding.

The Sun King himself, the biggest star-
I admire you from afar,
lost in this palace of shimmering gold

there is no end in sight- it all looks the same.
These pieces are protected at all costs.
They carry so much meaning,

so much strength and power...
that it had to crumble-
had to be reborn.

Like the flowers that bloom each spring,
whose fragile beauty remains unseen,
longing to be adored by many-

I feel this in my soul, in my dreams-
my heart is filled with love and beauty.
I wish to project my feelings on others-

to not feel alone

to not feel lost

to be complete.

— Mary-Anne, Kassidy, & Kendall

MR You stand in a garden of endless beauty
Your bold stances tells me you belong here

Your smile tells me you know a secret
And through these paintings I can hear your story
KR These rooms so full of life and laughter
with so much history between these walls

KS I carry the weight on my shoulders
thinking of all possibilities that could happen at anytime
like a star exploding

MR The Sun King himself, the biggest star
I admire you from afar
Lost in this palace of glimmering gold
there is no end in sight it all looks the same
KR these peices are protected at all costs
they carry so much meaning

KS So much strength and power
that it had to require me
had to be reborn

MR Like the flowers that bloom each spring
Whose fragile beauty remains unseen
Longing to be adored by many
I feel this in my soul in my dreams
KR my heart is with love and beauty
filled

I wish to project my feelings on others

KS To not feel alone
To not feel lost
To be complete.

Kendall Josten
Mary-Anne Ramirez

Artists being Artists— scarcely a more enchanting sight in all of Paris...

Kendall

Te quiero
ASSAVAKKIT
Ndikukonda
je t'aime
Saya cinta padamu

I am not a writer
I am not an artist I say
as I walk along the cobblestone streets of Paris
I am surrounded by people who exude artistry
beauty
magic
I watch as words flow from their fingertips
Scribbles becoming drawings
Words becoming powerful poems

How? I ask myself
How are these wonderful artists able to create from thin air?
How are they able to look at something
and have a whole world mapped out in their minds?
I feel like a fraud amongst them
These people who believe whole-heartedly in themselves,
Maybe that's what I need to do
believe in myself
Easier said than done I suppose,
But I have to say the one phrase Rachel taught me
No matter what...

I am a poet

je suis poète

KENDALL JOSTEN

95

"Let's dance," he says.

I don't dance.

I don't know how.

I don't know how to just let loose and

let the music wash over me.

My thoughts racing through my mind

of how embarrassing I would look if I tried.

He takes my hand and says, "Look into my eyes.

There is a neon sign in a Champagne cellar

in Reims that says 'Dance first, think later'.

What do you say we do that tonight?"

I shake my head, smiling at the silliness.

"Okay," I say as we walk to the dance floor.

I look around me. At the bodies swaying and writhing,

everyone lost in the music.

In their own worlds.

I take a deep breath, close my eyes and start to dance.

dansez d'abord,
réfléchissez plus tard

KENDALL JOSTEN

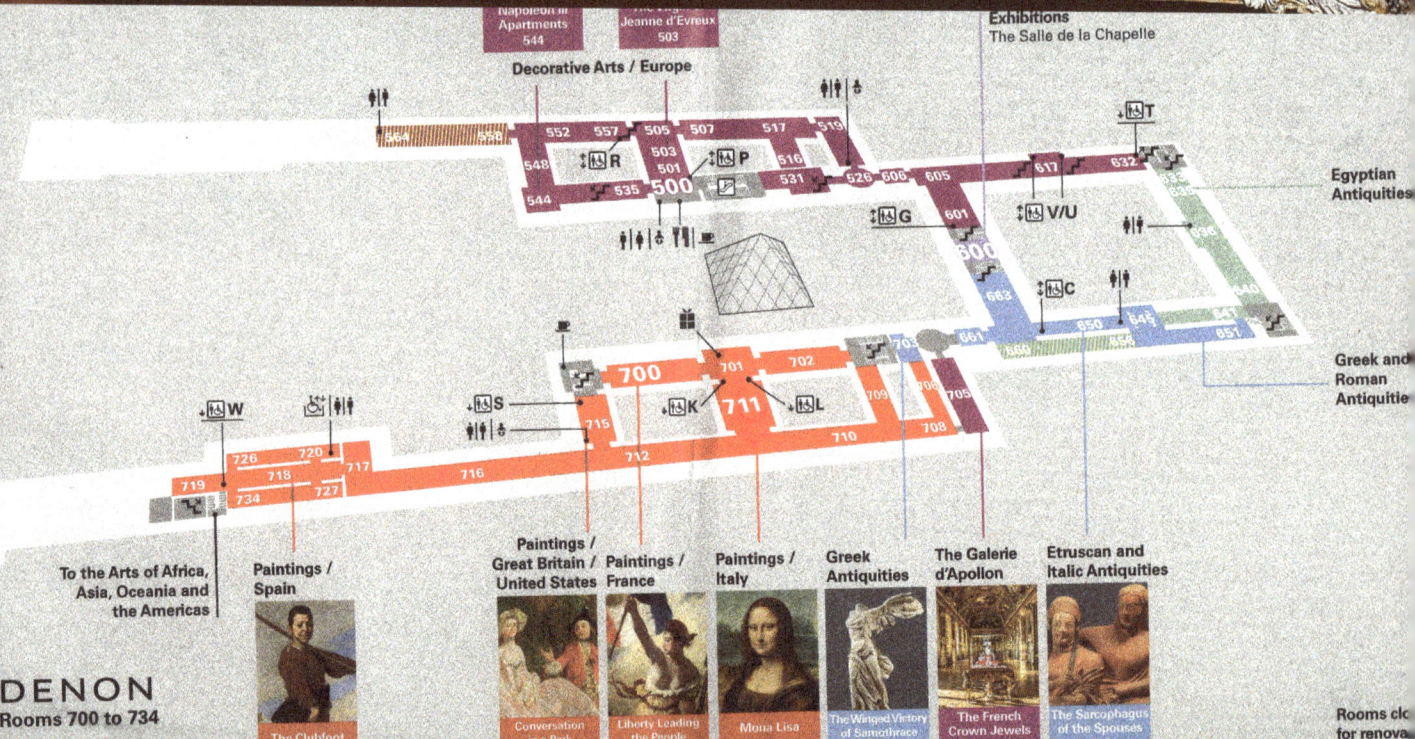

Napoleon III
Apartments
544

The
Jeanne d'Evreux
503

Exhibitions
The Salle de la Chapelle

Decorative Arts / Europe

552 557   505 507   517 519

548   503   516   Egyptian
501   Antiquities

544   535 500   531   626 606 605   617   632

G   601   V/U

500

663   C

661

700   701 702

711   709

715   712   710   708   705

K   L   Greek and
Roman
Antiquitie

726 720
719   717
718   716
734 727

**To the Arts of Africa,
Asia, Oceania and
the Americas**

**Paintings /
Spain**

**Paintings /
Great Britain /
United States**

**Paintings /
France**

**Paintings /
Italy**

**Greek
Antiquities**

**The Galerie
d'Apollon**

**Etruscan and
Italic Antiquities**

DENON
Rooms 700 to 734

The Clubfoot

Conversation
in a Park

Liberty Leading
the People

Mona Lisa

The Winged Victory
of Samothrace

The French
Crown Jewels

The Sarcophagus
of the Spouses

Rooms clc
for renova

The architecture speaks to me.
Telling me their history
of war and revolution,
of fanfare and misery.
What would it be like to walk amongst the streets,
unknown.
The song within the walls reaching out,
humming their tune.
Trying to tell me the stories of what once was.
A hall of mirrors within a golden palace.
Liberty Leading the People on a wall in the Louvre.
Unnoticed by most,
but fierce.
What power these elements have to the people of the city.
What magic is shown through art and history,
storytelling the way the world was and where it is going.
To see the world through an artist's eye
would be something magical indeed.

Did *Mona Lisa* ever smile?

ce qui était autrefois n'est plus

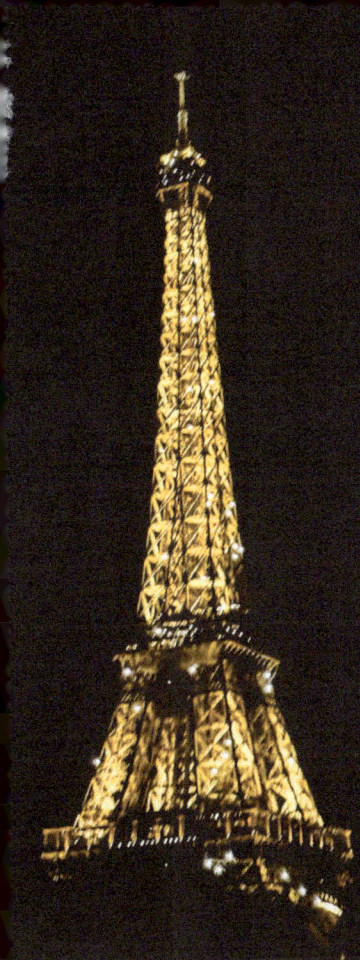

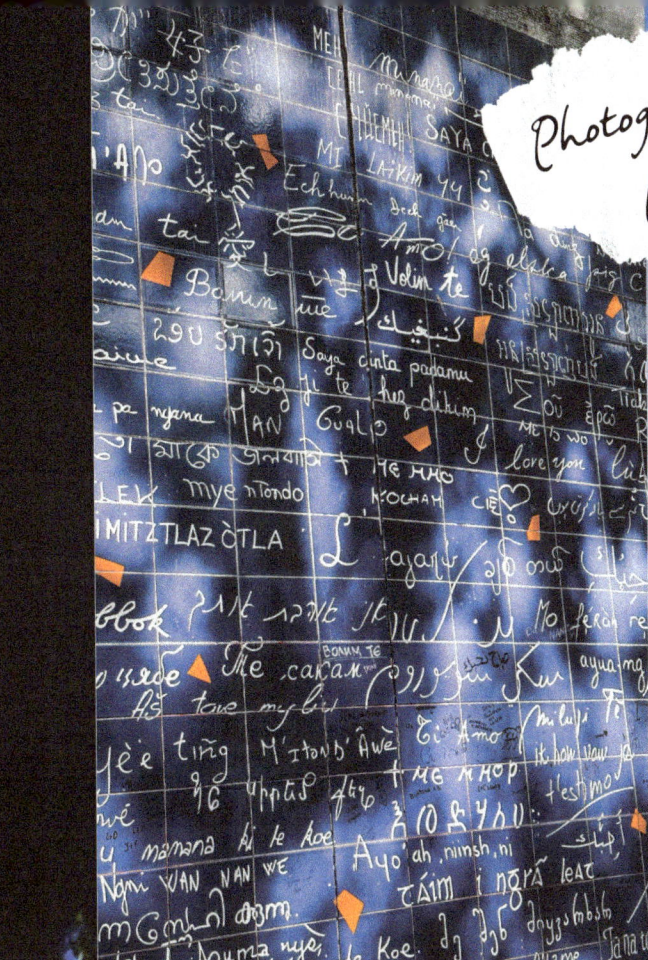

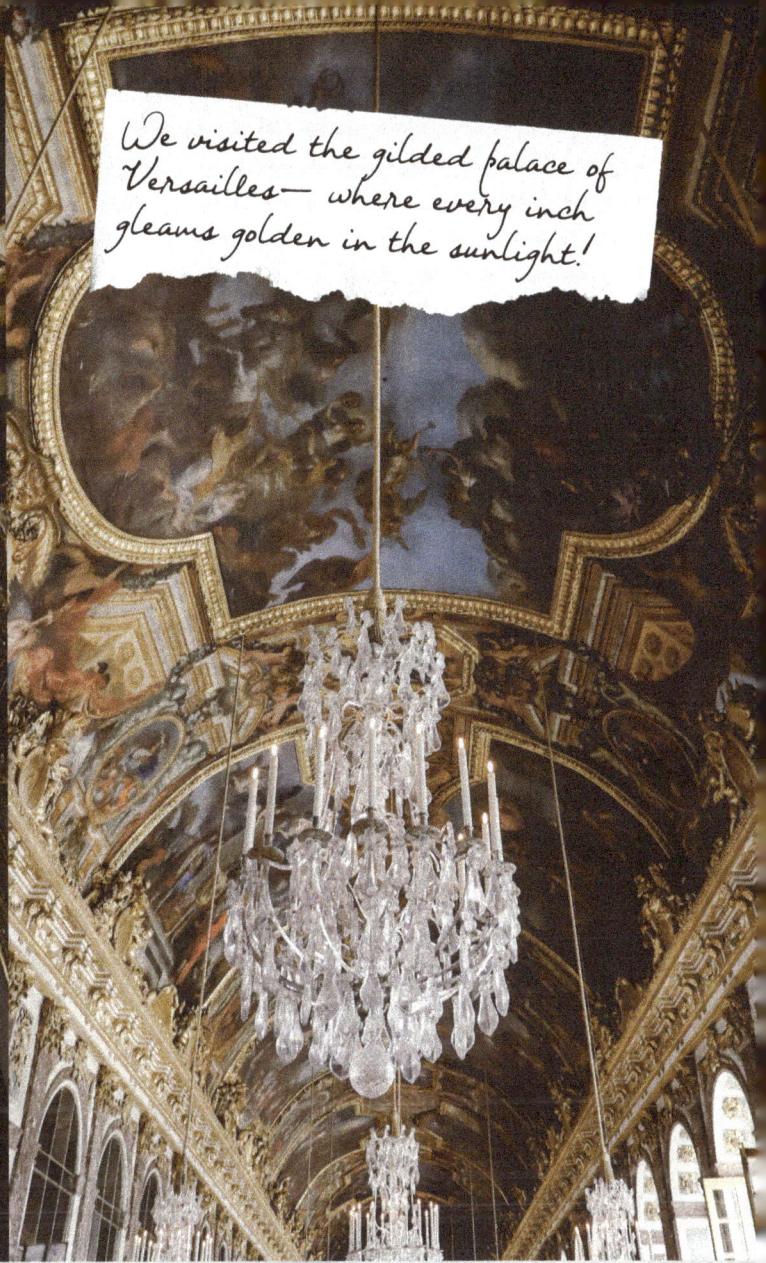

We visited the gilded palace of Versailles— where every inch gleams golden in the sunlight!

PETIT TRIANON

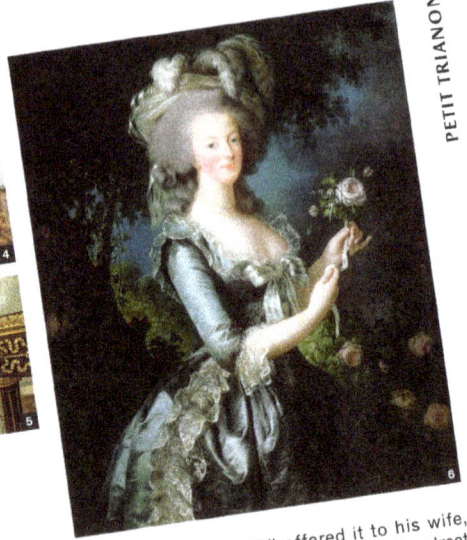

The neo-Greek-style Petit Trianon prefigured a return to the antique and neo-classical style in the late 18th century. The decision by Louis XV, who had moved into the Grand Trianon in 1750, to install new, more private areas, led to the creation of the French Pavilion – a small summer dining room built by Ange-Jacques Gabriel in 1750 and completed by the addition of the Cool Pavilion in 1753. These buildings, erected in the French Garden – one of the last of this style – were surrounded by a menagerie and a kitchen garden, where the King was able to sample farm produce.

The Marquise de Pompadour urged the King to block off the view of the garden by building a new palace, the Petit Trianon, which was built between 1761 and 1768 by Ange-Jacques Gabriel. This extremely cramped palace was initially occupied by the Countess Du Barry, who had become the King's new favourite following the death of Madame de Pompadour, in 1764.

"You like flowers, so I have a bouquet for you: Petit Trianon."

Louis XVI to Marie-Antoinette

1. View of the Petit Trianon from the French Garden

2. Queen's Bedchamber

3. Temple of Love

4. Reception Room

5. "Movable Mirrors" Boudoir

6. Portrait of *Marie-Antoinette with rose* (1755-1793), by Élisabeth Louise Vigée Le Brun (1755-1842), oil on canvas

In 1774, King Louis XVI offered it to his wife, Marie-Antoinette, who made it her private retreat and completely transformed the gardens, creating a single, Anglo-Chinese-style garden with a grotto, waterfall and various small buildings. It was accomplished by her architect, Richard Mique, whose construction of the Queen's Hamlet, between 1783 and 1786, was his crowning achievement. Thus, not far from the palace, the Queen had a place of relaxation and enjoyment, including a small private theatre.

We strolled through the Petit Trianon, a peaceful retreat where neoclassical elegance and nature's whisper blend in perfect harmony

We paused at the Temple of Love, a delicate marble haven where romance and tranquility meet...

Midsummer Muses

We are the quiet ones,
in a sea of noise-
our breath soft as
a french perfume,
toes in the grass and
eyes darting from sky
to page- the sound
of ink pen and paintbrush
sweeping across blank
space- we are the
observers, the memory
keepers, the admirers, the
seers of unnoticeable things-
we are the artists- and in
the midst of chaos, we are
tranquility.

— R. Clift

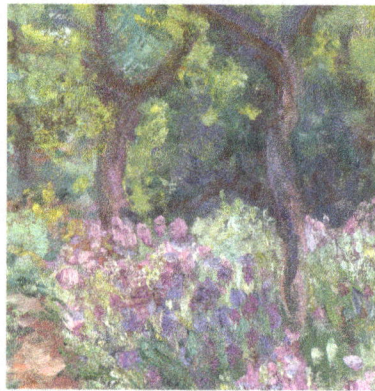

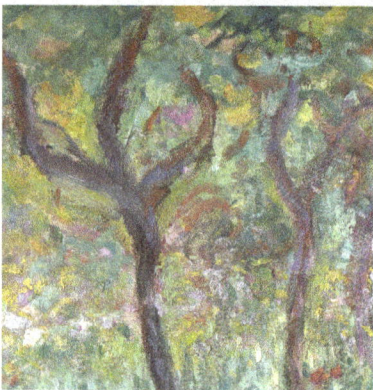

Leisly

untitled poem I

it was clear, from the very first day
- *or rather the second* -
a presence that beckoned remembrance
the way that red dress weaved through
the streets of an unknown city
and beckoned
unmistakable safety ;
we toured Montmarte, the Sacré-Cœur,
and even The Louvre that day
I walked through centuries and traversed entire lifetimes
and when the sun rose again and the wardrobe changed to an
alarming shade of black
- *so synonymous with out of sight* -
and I could no longer spot you through the people,
through the monuments,
through the lifetimes,
even then
I knew better than to fear ;
I saw you abandon those pull-apart eyeglasses
to try on a pair of bright yellow children's sunglasses
bore witness to you being caught in perplexity
by the mere concept
of *"Bubble Tea"*
and then enamored
by the prospect of future freebies
all the while carrying yourself
with a spirit of adventure
amongst a group of strangers
that looked to you, begging for guidance ;

it was clear from the very first day
you see
that I was in complete and utter
unfamiliar territory
like a small sailboat,
ill-equipped to brave the sea ;
you were ~~my~~ our lighthouse
and you've no idea how much that meant to me

       for Sylvie   LEISLY ROMAN

I found comfort in

the collective wonder / the independence / the silliness of her
- / *the youngest, freest of us all* - / the accented voices of
passersby that reminded me / *I am in the midst of a once-in-a-
lifetime journey* / a stranger's guidance / who found her way /
into the folds of my fragile heart / and in every rogue flake of
croissant / that when lifted from the plate / broke apart / in
resistance / *as I did from my very own host that week* / the safety
in him - / for *what a gift it is to travel with those who are
well-versed* / *in health, yes, but in benevolence, even more* - /
alleyways adorned in ~~graffiti~~ street art / precious ~~structures~~
history admired by ~~crowds~~ curious souls / every bloom of every
color - / *no shade of flower I don't adore* - / a musical man
/ a portable fan / the fact that I, Leisly Ann, endeavored to
believe herself when she said "*You can*" / being on the opposite
side of the lens, for once - / *that's what she does, you know* /
cultivates a cocoon of confidence that is anything but pixelated
- / the sound of my mother's voice when I called to say goodnight
/ every night / followed by my subsequent smile and apology soon
after / everytime / as I remembered / *the evening song has not
yet been sung* / back home - / my <u>discomfort</u>, my <u>uncertainty</u>, my
own <u>internal strifes</u> / because deep down I knew I deserved these
moments / *and I was going to be alright*

untitled poem II

how many ways can one say "I love you?"

dozens, hundreds perhaps

how many languages must one perfect?

they needn't master any dialect,
only the metronome of another one's soul

how many times should I utter the words,
to make certain they don't forget?

the heart does not rely on memory love, it relies,
on synchronicity

SAYA CINTA PADAMU
MI LAIKIM YU
I love you
Ndagukunda
nalligivagit
yèe tiŋg
M'itond' Awe
35
35A
36
36A

untitled poem III

how many of us would burn
the skin off our bones
until it resembled the most perfect piece of parchment

repurpose our own blood
once coursing through our very veins
as ink – *let it bring life to the page instead*

dress the walls of every street and alleyway
because alas
the halls of every known structure will never be enough

frame our darkest selves and then ask to be hung
in the light, where at least then we could exist as a muse –
how many of us yearn, yearn to be seen, as poetry

LEISLY ROMAN

they call it the "City of Love"
for acceptance is engraved here -
in the walls
in the stone
in the hearts of its community ;
and there is a faint yet evident scent
that seems to line even the cracks in the street -
it smells welcoming
as if to say
*"Your soul is safe here, I tell you,
feel free to please stay."*

TRANS IS BEAUTIFUL ♡

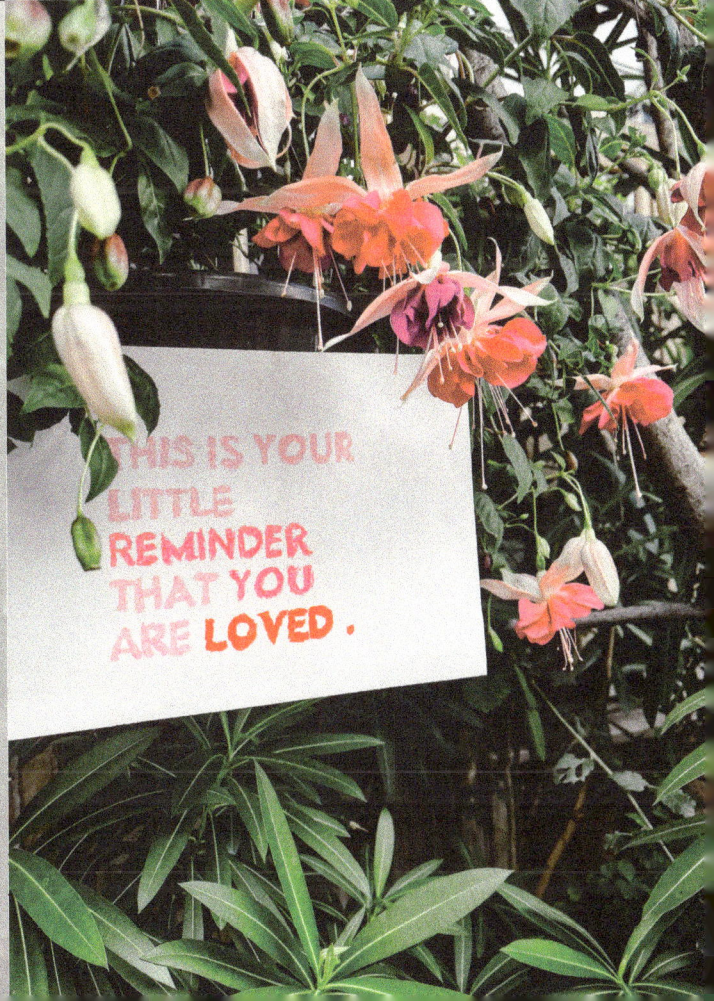

THIS IS YOUR LITTLE REMINDER THAT YOU ARE LOVED.

untitled poem IV

Where does it lead?
This I do not know
Though wherever it is
This is where I must go ;

I needn't a key
To set myself free
I only needed to believe -
Believe in the strength, in me

untitled poem V

the flame of this city
may flicker
but never wanes -
there is distinct beauty here
amongst
the mundane

"Go On"

i board a plane and pray
and pray
and pray
i only wish to land
and as the wheels meet the ground
my desires, they shift
for now i only wish to stand
the fear, the distance, at the very least up out of this seat ;

Lapis Lazuli hangs from my chest for protection
along with a rosary gifted to me by my father's friend
— my father says it was blessed by the Pope himself
so as you can see, i've pulled out all the stops —
i boarded a plane and it landed, it made it
snapped a photo for my mother to show her i was alright
and then before the very last drip of nerve drops
inhale, exhale, the very first step, is now done

LEISLY ROMAN

untitled tanka

crippled from within

to the point of no return -

seemingly, for the

whispers shouted *"no," "danger"*

but *you did it anyway*

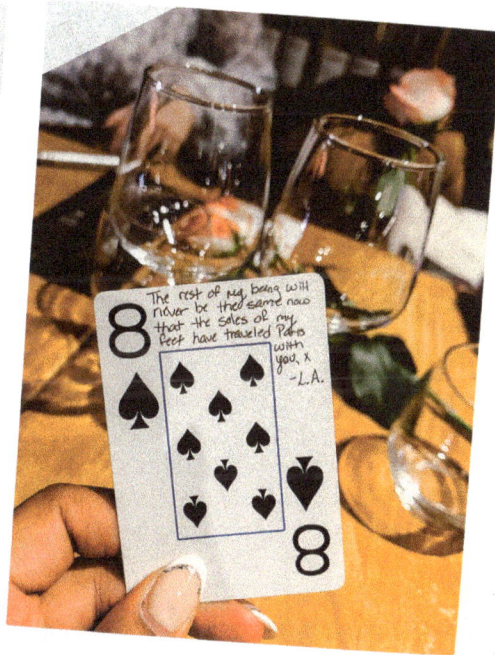

The rest of my being will
never be the same now
that the soles of my
feet have traveled Paris
with
you. x
~L.A.

"BE NOT INHOSPITABLE TO STRANGERS LEST THEY BE ANGELS IN DISGUISE"
- a quote I read atop a doorway at the Shakespeare & Co bookstore
we went to today.

We have one of these in my city but I've only been in there for
academic reasons. Textbooks and miscellaneous supplies to survive
(hopefully) 4 years of undergrad. Stuff like that. I'm pretty sure
this was my first time going into a Shakespeare & Co, and actually
taking the time to take it all in. The sound of the floorboards
as I move slowly through the rows of shelves, the feeling of the
countless felt and velvet chairs and what I swear looked like beds
inherited straight from the Renaissance (I think I tried to sit
on every one of them), the titles of classics I've yet to read but
who've nevertheless inspired me, if anything, with how well they've
aged.

I think the first floor was for browsing and book buying while the
second floor was for reprieve. Exploration. Simply experiencing,
and being. I climbed the discolored stairs with a new friend with
one intention - I was going to leave a copy of my book here. Someone
would hopefully find it. Flip open to the little note I wrote on one
of the first pages. Maybe take the book home with them, once they
realized there was no price sticker, and that it likely wasn't part
of the infamous bookstore's inventory. That pretty much means it's
up for grabs, right? Surely someone would think this way...

I placed a copy of my collection on one of the soft benches or beds
or whatever kind of seating it was, and of course in true tourist
fashion, recorded every second of it from the walk over to the
placing of it down to the walk back. I thought it would be special
to look back on. My book in Paris, who would've thought! I turn
around, pick up the stack of books that I most definitely did not
need but most definitely was not leaving without, and let my friend
know I was done with my silly little idea. I wasn't though. Not
once I saw what I saw once we started to make our way back to the
worn stairway. My book, in someone's hands, already. I asked my
friend if we could sit. I just wanted to watch for a little while.
Maybe that was creepy, but I could not just leave. I wouldn't have
seen them flip through the pages with a pensive look on their face.
I would've missed when they called their friend over and started
showing them some pages. They sat together, read together, read my
book together. I couldn't help but think "Wow." And "Why?" And "Oh
my God." The quote. It came true.

I've never heard of Sylvia Beach before today. Not once, I don't
think. Can you imagine? Owing an inconceivable amount of thanks to
a person whose name has yet to take up even 1 square foot of space
in your brain, despite how neverending it sometimes feels? I like
to think the remedy for that is travel. New and unknown does not
have to stay new and unknown. I am sorry Miss Beach. But I am also,
so very thankful for you.

LEISLY ROMAN

—————

- L.A. x

BE NOT INHOSPITABLE TO STRANGERS
LEST THEY BE ANGELS IN DISGUISE

SYLVIA BEACH 1887~1962
FOUNDER OF THE FIRST
SHAKESPEARE & Cº 1919~1941
HALF BOOKSTORE AND HALF
LENDING LIBRARY. HER PATRONS
INCLUDED ERNEST HEMINGWAY,
GERTRUDE STEIN, JANET FLANNER
F. SCOTT FITZGERALD, DJUNA BARNES
AND T.S. ELIOT~ WRITERS FOR WHOM
SHE ACTED AS BANKER, POST OFFICE
AND FRIEND. SHE WAS THE FIRST
TO PUBLISH JAMES JOYCE'S
"ULYSSES" IN 1922, WHEN NO ONE
ELSE DARED. THE FRENCH
WRITER ANDRE CHAMSON SAID
THAT BEACH DID MORE TO LINK
ENGLAND, THE UNITED STATES,
IRELAND AND FRANCE THAN FOUR
GREAT AMBASSADORS COMBINED.

untitled poem VI

and it's astonishing really
the way we we utilize the Earth's gifts –
stone
marble
porcelain
gold –
as bounty ;

we create man-made structures that tower over
the men who worked tirelessly to perfect them
and if the royals of centuries past left for us
any particular lesson to consider
I believe that they'd note that lifeless things,
inanimate by nature –
statues, monuments, legacies –
though they cannot move, they will move you

LEISLY ROMAN

"Unintended Fruits"

I did not need to travel overseas
To experience reunion
I did not need to know the soil of a new land
For the blessing of heartfelt union ;

I did not need to come to Paris
To grant my soul a new shade of gleam
Though that's precisely what occurred
And I am eternally grateful, to have endured this living dream

LEISLY ROMAN

untitled poem VII

how serendipitous it is

growing wanderlust from the seeds of fear

creating art

with new souls now held dear

We roamed the vast gardens of Versailles, where symmetry and nature converge in endless beauty

Sometimes artists become the art

Sylvie bought us a pizza to share, turning an ordinary meal into a memorable moment together!

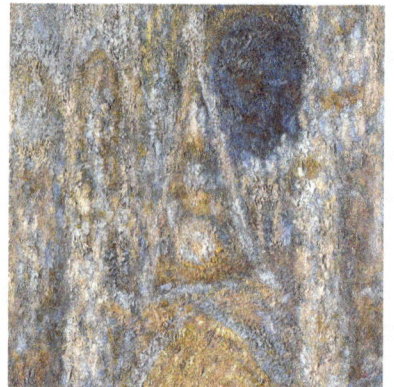

Mary-Anne

ARC DE TRIOMPHE

ARC DE TRIOMPHE
TARIF INDIV

TARIF INDIV

Valable le 07/07/2023

Vendu le 07/07/2023 à 19:21 NI ECHANGE NI REMBOURSE

C051/MERLE 2045165265375

13.00 EUR

Photo : Patrick CADET

Valable le 07/07/2023
Vendu le 07/07/2023 à 13:51
2045165265375

13.00 EUR

A Love Letter to Paris

I want to know you.
The real you.
Not the version I've seen in movies.
The city of love,
The city of lights,
Who are you really?
A pre-conceived notion, a fantasy?
I don't really know you.
The words "Paris is always a good idea,"
Echo through my naive brain.
Stepping into you is like meeting my favorite celebrity,
And they say you should never meet your heroes.
But I am intrigued by you.
Fascinated by the promise of hope you bring.
I've been warned about you.
Do you feel safe?
Your reputation precedes you.
The Eiffel Tower sparkles, your glimmering eyes.
The Seine River, your twisted smile.
The Arc de Triomphe, your welcoming arms.
It invites me in, makes me feel at home.
You are more than all of these things,
more than a place of beauty.
You are the mundane moments of lovers
drinking hot chocolate in cafes.
You are the group of poets laughing
as they devour a giant croissant.
You are couples dancing in the streets.
The people breathe life into you.
I yearn for that indescribable feeling of knowing you.
Tell me who you are or who you long to be.
For I am ready to immerse in you.

Mary-Anne Ramirez

These Words

Dear Paris,
I have no poem for you.
This is merely a collection of ideas,
Assembled like a puzzle with a missing piece.
This is not a story,
But rather an accumulation of concepts,
Borrowed thoughts assuming the form of originality.
This is not writing.
It is easily a late conversation between soul and creator.
A never ending list of unanswered questions.
This is not poetry.
It is only ink bleeding through the page.
A selection of letters and lines falling into place.
Stanzas accepting their fate.
An escape from the mundanity of day to day.
This is not love.
It is simply a seduction of phrases,
Cleverly curated like paintings in a museum.
I have no poem for you, but rather rantings of a beautiful
mind,
An excerpt of entertaining lies,
A documentation of existence of this moment in time.
This is not a poem.
It is ecstasy in words.

MARY-ANNE RAMIREZ

MARY-ANNE RAMIREZ

Distant Love

In the city of love,
And I left mine behind.
I see a couple kissing and holding hands.
Playfully dodging and laughing as they wait to cross
the street.
The wind blowing their hair,
Like they're the stars of some romantic movie,
That I've been given the pleasure of viewing from the
front row.
Oh, to be that in love.
So carelessly lost in their own world,
With no fear of cars and bikes flying by.
That should be me and mine.

MARY-ANNE RAMIR.

So Cute

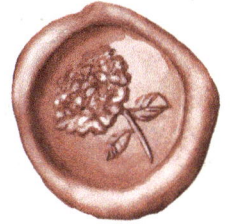

On our last night, we became more bonded than ever before.

We shared photos of our beloved pets at the dinner table.

The ooh's and aww's overpowering the restaurant ambiance.

The adorable four-legged creatures light up

on home screens and camera rolls.

The bittersweet promise of tomorrow still lingering

in the back of our minds,

But longing to be focused on this beautiful connection in time.

And somehow these dogs and cats united us.

We proclaim their names and tell silly stories.

We share memories of how they entered our lives.

They are in a way, an extension of who we are.

I suddenly see another side to the person across from me.

Some will return to those very animals in those still images,

And some will continue on to explore other lands.

A table of poets, so different but the one thing we have in common,

Is those precious souls waiting for us to eventually come home.

Hall of Mirrors

Golden reflections of past glimmering lives,
Present themselves so gracefully.
I look into the mirrors,
And who do I see?
A glimpse of royalty.
The body of a woman, who traveled so far,
To be introduced to the king and queen.
She wears a dress that blends
into the gardens of Versailles,
But does she really fit in?
Or is it just an illusion?
This modern princess knows not of
tight corsets and fancy jewels.
Try as she might, she doesn't belong here.
She'll forever remain,
An observer, like the statues in the garden.
Preserved in time,
Forever viewing the palace from the outside.

MARY-ANNE RAMIREZ

The Garden

We became flowers,

Under the French sun.

Blossomed into an arrangement,

Of different colors and sizes.

We created a garden far more beautiful,

Than Versailles.

MARY-ANNE RAMIREZ

The Moon and The Sun

If I am the moon,

Then, dear, you are the sun.

Your love burns with passion.

You rise with grace,

And set gently in hues of red.

My heart is waxing and waning,

Longing to be full.

You chase after me,

And I you.

We are 93 million miles apart,

Yet I feel no distance.

I envy the way your rays shine so bright,

And give life to those below.

You envy the way my very being can move tides.

When I fall, you stand tall.

You are my light,

You are my star.

My sun,

Your moon.

Beautifully apart,

Better when we lay together,

Eclipsing the earth.

MARY-ANNE RAMIREZ

Starlight

By the light of the sun,
Do not let me forget,
Those souls I've grown to love.
Starlight, star bright,
Those poets who shined brighter than the moon at night.
Each of us like stars in the sky,
Arranged in this moment in time.
We became a new constellation,
One that Orion would envy.
And it's no coincidence,
It's fate, call it destiny.
We are burning and fading,
In this iridescent galaxy.
We will soon travel new paths.
Become lost in our own worlds.
Discover a new universe,
Remembering the stars we once called home.

Victory

She is victorious.

Her winged stance exudes,

Power and grace.

I've never seen such beauty and mystery.

She is strength and fragility.

She stands tall,

Admired by all who long to understand her,

All who lay at her feet.

MARY-ANNE RAMIREZ

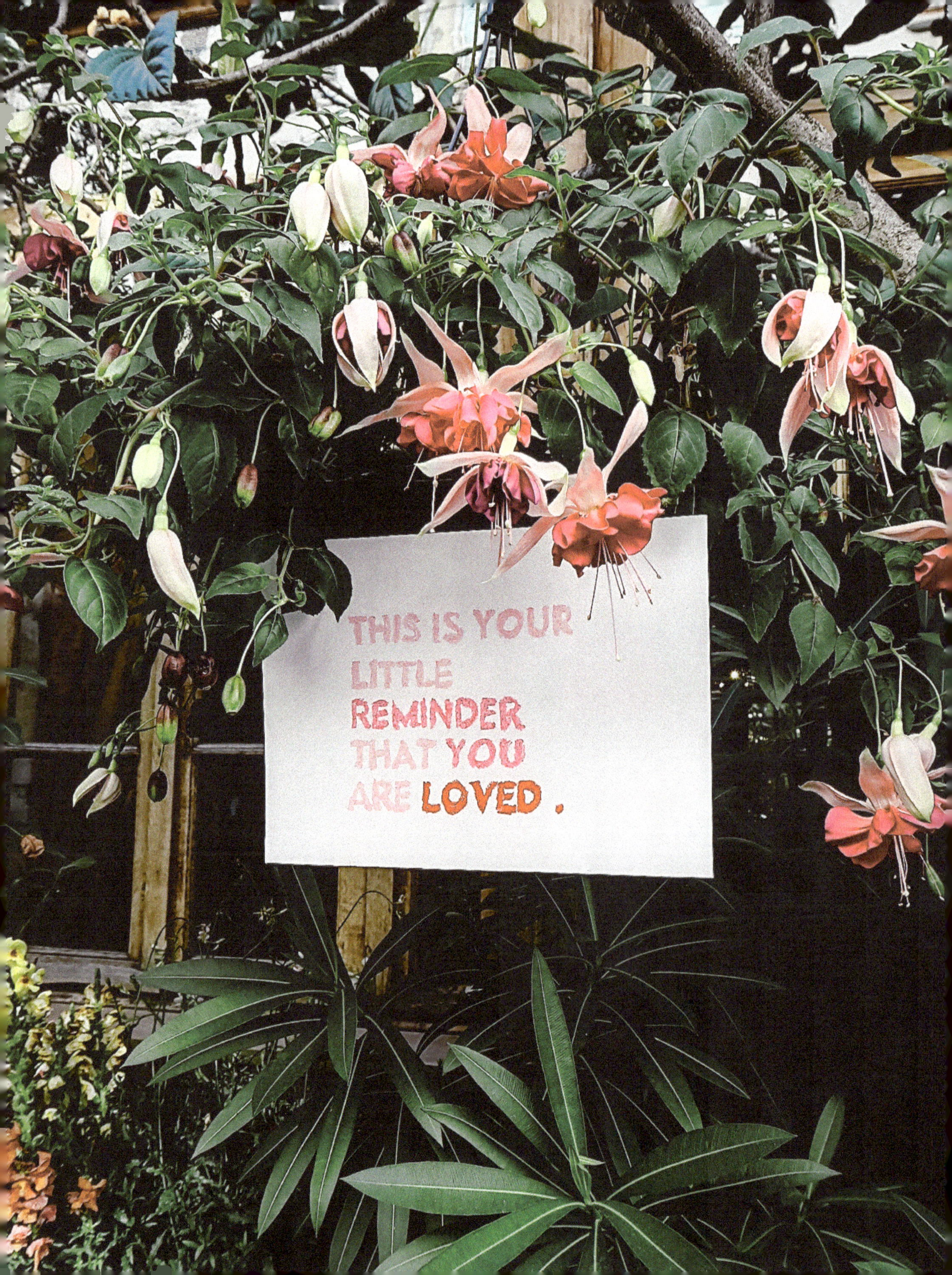
THIS IS YOUR
LITTLE
REMINDER
THAT YOU
ARE LOVED.

This is Your Little Reminder That You Are Loved

How perpetually adored I was,
By all I encountered.
The vision of perfection to new eyes,
An untold story to new minds.
Fresh air to those who had yet to breathe me in.
I was any version of myself that they wanted me to be,
Until I open my mouth and they see...
The true me,
Or the me I want them to know.
I feel shiny and new here.
I wish to stay in this place that welcomes all of me.
The signs remind me that I'm loved.
How cherished was I,
Simply for my presence,
My mere existence.
I want to be like a freshly opened gift.
A ray of sunshine,
A flower that blooms with pure delight,
Forever treasured.

MARY-ANNE RAMIREZ

I Wish

There are poems I wish I had written.
Words I wish were created in my mind.
Sentences I wish I had constructed.
Ideas I wish I gave life to.
There are paintings I wish I had made,
Colors I decided to blend together.
Art deemed worthy of a museum.
I wish the words and art
were born within my brain,
To exist in the world,
To be the first of its kind.

We're Looking at You

Packaging baked goods,

The Parisian woman cuts tape with her teeth.

The tour guide calls her out,

"This is not home,

This is a bakery."

The woman is unaware,

She has observers.

Viewing her through a window

that frames her like a screen,

Foreigners, explorers on a bus,

Discovering a true mastermind at work.

MARY-ANNE RAMIREZ

Mona Lisa

Your eyes are captivating,
Luring me in.
Your smile tells me you know a secret,
I want to know.
There is distance between us,
A river of people,
That ebb and flow.
Will we ever officially meet?
Or must I continue to admire you from afar?
I have traveled a long way,
To gaze upon your gaze.
To discover the reason you are so adored.
For such a small frame,
You have such a large presence.
A devoted audience.
It was nice to see you,
Like checking in on an old friend.

MARY-ANNE RAMIREZ

The Rose

I leave a rose behind,
One gifted to me on my last night.
White with a touch of pink,
Like a kiss that has faded over time.
I wish I could take her with me,
To accompany me on my travels,
Or even back home.
I leave the white-pink rose behind,
For some other worthy soul to find.

MARY-ANNE RAMIREZ

Go(gh)

My dearest Vincent,
I now see what you see.
The way the light reflects on the Seine,
The circles and swirls,
And swatches in hues of blue.
I am now you.
Your painting has come to life,
Before my very eyes.
The waves dance like the couples on the streets.
The tower beams proudly in the distance.
My love hands me a figure in your likeness and says "Go,"
Go out there and make art like Van Gogh.
So I take you with me,
To Paris, your home.
I visit the places you've once graced with your presence,
And long to capture the beauty of this world
like you once did.

MARY-ANNE RAMIREZ

Cheers

You became wine,
In the richness,
And the tartness,
And the addiction.
I poured you into my cup.
I see you as half full.
Something so simple,
That I grew to love.
I grew to need.
You then became champagne,
In the bubbly-ness,
And the sweetness,
And the fixation.
You soon became cold.
Like a dark cellar at night,
Where I store my resentment.

The White Butterfly

The white butterfly follows me.

A guardian angel on my shoulder.

She rests her wings on the flowers,

In my garden of hope.

How effortlessly she goes,

Delicate, yet making her presence known.

A reminder of the peace and serenity I seek.

Rain, Rain

In the absence of the sun,

We found love in the rain.

The stormy clouds that hover over us,

Give birth to drops that quench our faces.

We see the true beauty of Paris,

Amongst the dark and gloom.

The city of lights floods our minds,

As the streets fill up with water,

And the people rush to get inside.

Sun rays peek through the gray,

As vivid colors begin to appear.

In the presence of the sun,

We found hope again.

Mary-Anne Ramirez

Abuela/The Beret

The image of my grandmother,
Is not one that most people would think.
I have a decade of memories with her,
And I only remember half of it.
Mi abuela,
A woman who often dreamed of Paris.
She wears a beret to keep her head warm.
She never made it there, but I did.
The woman who always told me to put on a hat
when it was cold outside.
My earliest memory is wearing a beret
and playing with her in the snow.
When I land in Paris, I scour through souvenir shops.
I come across the cliche that is the beret,
And I immediately reject it.
This piece of constructed fabric,
This itchy wool,
It's all I have left of her.
The memory is too painful,
And my hands tremble as I cling on to it.
I let it go.
As I leave the shop, I receive a phone call,
It's my mother, my grandmother's daughter.
My mom asks me to buy a beret for her,
I think to myself, "Why wouldn't I get one?"
It's what she would've wanted.
I go back to the souvenir shop.
I admire the different colors of berets,
And I am reminded of how far I've come.
I have made her dream come true,
By simply being here.
I buy one for my mother and one for myself,
And I pack them along with the postcards
and magnets I've collected.
When I look at a beret I don't think of Paris,
I think of my grandmother,
And of the love she had for me.

MARY-ANNE RAMIREZ

Memories

Viewing a new city like a child,
Through fresh eyes, a new perspective.
We became little kids again.
Suddenly it was easy to make a friend.
Show and tell of the gifts we bought,
Giggling behind the bus,
Playing hopscotch in a park,
Lost in this moment.
Carelessly our true selves.
We discover things we've learned in books.
We write, we draw, we nap.
This will all soon fade into a memory,
Of silly photos and witty jokes.
We hope our paths will cross again,
And that these beautiful moments we've shared,
Will forever bind us.

MARY-ANNE RAMIREZ

Par Amour/For Love

I see the declarations of a man's love for his wife,

All over the city,

And I long to be admired in that way.

I yearn for a man who will express his adoration,

For all eyes to see -

Me,

The keeper of his heart,

His ever-loving muse.

I dream that he would paint little hearts on forbidden walls.

To break the rules,

All in the name of love.

MARY-ANNE RAMIREZ

Photographay by
Mary-Anne Ramirez

Paris Montmartre

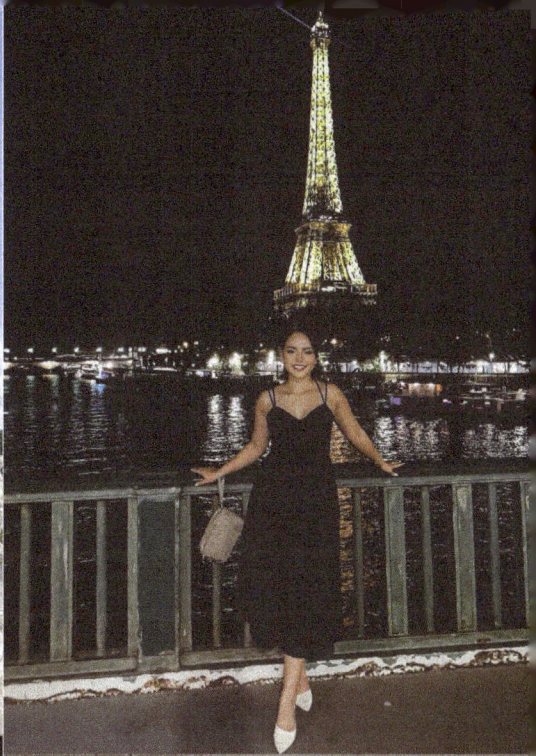
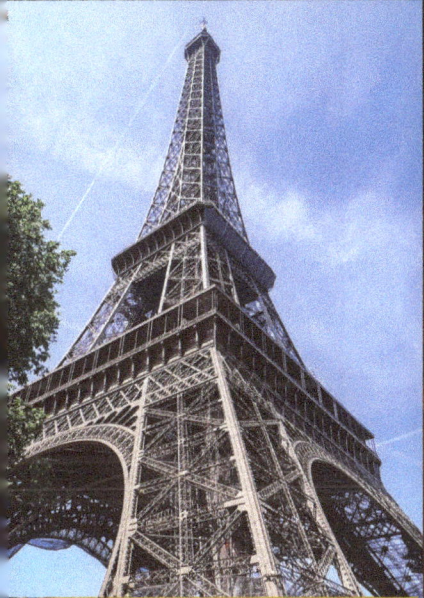

l'amour
est clair comme le jour,
l'amour
est simple comme le bonjour,
l'amour
est nu comme la main,
c'est ton amour et le mien

Jacques
Prévert

We toured a woman-founded Pommery, where the rich history of champagne unfolded in every cellar and glowing tunnel...

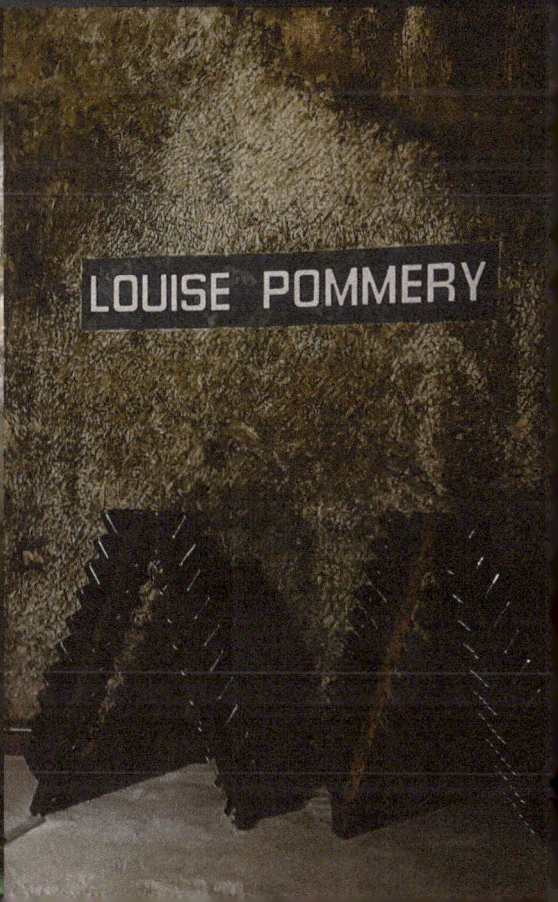

LOUISE POMMERY

The cellars were full of art installations— we felt like we had fallen into wonderland!

Sunshine

SUNSHINE ALEXANDRIA

Breathe

i n h a l e
. . . . .

i am learning to breathe
outside the boundaries
of my own ribcage

e x h a l e
. . . .

learning to let life
fill up my lungs
so deeply

i n h a l e
. . . . .

it feels like my entire being
is exuding oxygen

e x h a l e
. . . .

finally at peace
in letting go of control
and trusting the flow~

i n h a l e
. . . . .

existing in the world
just as a cloud in the sky~
as a river through the earth

e x h a l e
. . . .

*floating, flowing,
a human, being*

SUNSHINE ALEXANDRIA

The Broken Star

i traveled five thousand
miles from home
the furthest i have ever gone
hauling around
a broken heart
while the summer sun
wraps me in warmth

but i am still shivering
at my core
my feet they drag
it's all a bore
i cry and cry
too sad to fight
to just survive
i must survive

the darkness eats me
alive at night
i search for joy
and pray i'll find it

i lost my twinkle
my spark is gone
for i now expect
bad things to come

i cannot see
a way out of this
floating in a dark abyss
never struggled to this extent
lost inside my own silence

it hurts much worse
when i see myself
so miserable
it's clear to tell

SUNSHINE ALEXANDRIA

my head it hangs
my eyes fall low
my smile now fades
soon as it comes

i hope the stars
don't judge my heart
for forgetting how to shine,
i promise i've not always been this way
i promise
i really
am trying

SUNSHINE ALEXANDRIA

Fireflies

it is unfair
that such beauty and bliss
as this exists,
but all you could see
was darkness.
i want to bring you back
and show you the light...

if life was a cave
deep underground
and this very moment
was a single firefly,
just this brief glimpse of light
would be enough
to illuminate the dark
for a lifetime~

you deserved to hold
every firefly in this world,
and i wish
i could have given
them all
to you

The Truth

To be honest:

i am here
to tell you *the truth*
and it may not be what you wish to read—
but the truth is;
travel can not always be
starlight & synchronicities—

the reality of life is,
you can and you will
endure times of darkness
wherever you may be
and though it can feel terrifying,
the light will return again.

you must know:
no matter how far away you go,
you can not outrun yourself—
and if *it is* adventure you seek
it is adventure you will find,
but perhaps not exactly the type
of adventure you had in mind~

see, the further away you go,
the deeper you go within;
exploring dark caves alone
deep inside your own chest
climbing the walls built tall
so your fragile heart wouldn't fall
and the pathway back to your soul
runs parallel, like a river
along your scars

you will discover so much
from the real journey, *within*
so embrace every challenge,
every moment,
every emotion~
even when
it hurts

SUNSHINE ALEXANDRIA

Compass

i hope you choose to leave behind
that place that doesn't feel much like home anymore;
that job that doesn't bring you joy anymore-
those people committed to misunderstanding you.
any place, any thing, and anyone
that makes you feel
like so much less
than you are.

carry with you
the lessons you've learned...
your self-worth,
the art of letting go
& a conscious understanding
of the preciousness of it all~
honor the ones you've lost
through fully living-
remember,
your time here too,
is limited

may you dig up the grave of hope
buried deep within your tired soul;
muster up the strength,
pack up all of the fear,
bring it all with you
in pursuit of
your happiness,
your dreams-
your life worth living...
because sometimes in life,
we must do it scared, tired, lost

listen to your inner calling,
the whisper deep within-

follow, as it guides you
to where you are meant to be~
to where your soul belongs
and your heart sings

i promise,
when you choose to follow
your inner compass
you will indeed
soar high
with wonder
and fly

SUNSHINE ALEXANDRIA

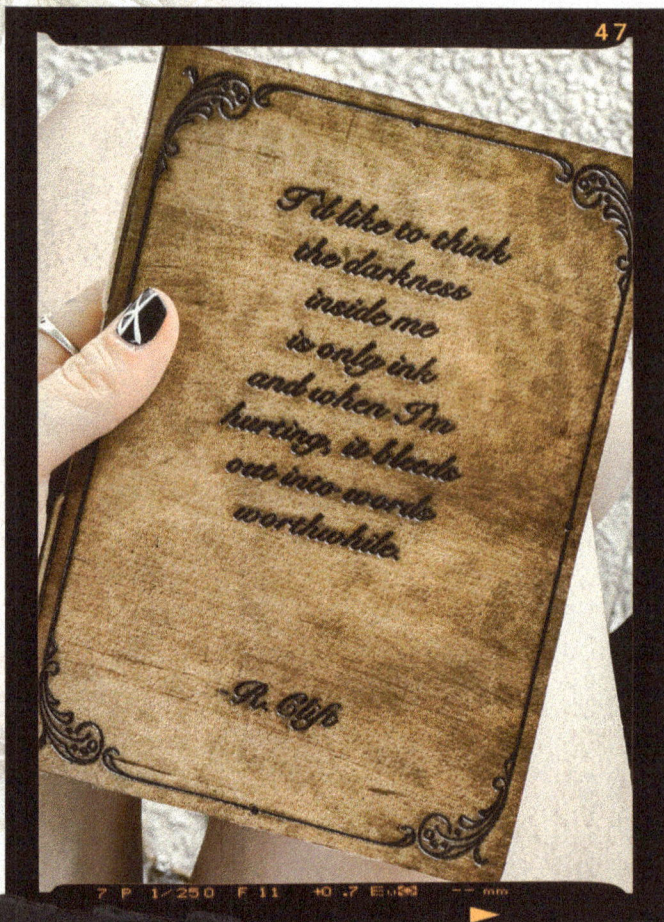

I'd like to think
the darkness
inside me
is only ink
and when I'm
hurting, it bleeds
out into words
worthwhile.

-R. Clift

the stars
are proof
that beauty can exist
in even
the darkest of places
-s.a.

Vers Luisants

he speaks so eloquently
in his native tongue,
with soft, imperfect english–

in the dead of night in giverny,
we wandered old, empty streets
through alleyways of cobblestone and hydrangeas–
lamp posts illuminating us in yellow light
in between gaps of darkness

we laughed as we walked,
sharing our stories
and learning each other's language,
building a new, international friendship–
our arms in an unbreakable chain
an instant bond of familiarity

then, suddenly
we were stopped in our tracks
by tiny, bioluminescent lights
scattered across a dark, open field

like a lake
reflecting the stars
in the night sky...

we stood together,
stunned in silence
and i could have sworn
i heard the glow worms
say, *"bonjour,"*

as city lights glimmered
in the distance

SUNSHINE ALEXANDRIA

The Badge

i remember you silencing me
with your scalding hot tongue
flicking,
explosive words like lava
eyes glowing red orange
mouth spewing embers of hatred
each word burning into my skin so deep,
you charred my heart.
"having dead friends isn't a badge of honor,"
as if it's one i'd like to wear...

i know,
this grief is embedded into my flesh-
body stitched together, like sally
each of my limbs just a part of someone i once knew.
and this badge you imagined-
well, it's left gaping holes in my chest
and a permanent mark so deep,
my skin could never push it out.
like a tattoo i *never* asked for.

in a way, you were right.
i know i wear this pain on my sleeve,
this translucent body, so vulnerable,
heart on display for all to see
i'm just living f r a g m e n t s
of all the people i've lost.
sometimes, i don't know where they end
and i begin.
this grief has been wound and wound
so tight around
every fiber of my being
for so much of my life,
i struggle to remember who i was
before it paralyzed me

so don't you <u>dare</u> act
like when i share *my* story
it makes *your* skin crawl...
you have no idea how it feels
to live within this battered body;
to have loved and lost *them all*.

SUNSHINE ALEXANDRIA

his laugh, her smile, their eyes;
endless conversations playing in my mind
on a never ending loop~

you don't understand what it's like
to be forced to carry
the heavy suitcase that is grief,
and the latches are broken,
and it keeps flying open
no matter how hard you try
to keep it shut.

you have never known a loss so agonizing,
that you, *yourself* became the ghost
when the only thing that can fill
the sunken void within your chest
is the presence of the very people
whom you will *never* see again.

so many, *so close*
and i find them in everything-
every day, constantly reminded
whether i see
the familiar smile of a stranger
standing in the grocery store,
or when i catch my own eyes
in the mirror and realize
i inherited his sadness.
the breeze blows a certain way
and my mind floods with memories;
and i can't outrun the wind.

so let me be the one
to extinguish
your fire breathing lungs
and silence
your sharpened tongue

you may not wish
to taste my tears,
but be grateful
that it is not *you*
who weeps them

conversation. Not that I don't trust you, of course,
you
answer such questions except in person,
are
a
That noted, I must confess that the unexpected
receipt of your correspondence via Ms. Vliegenthart
wondrous thing
even if
feel
i
n
g
frail
of that novel was so thin comparatively
optimistic.

Should you find yourself in Amsterdam,
however, please do pay a visit at your leisure. I am
usually home. I would even allow you a peek at my
grocery lists.

- pâtes feuilletées
- yaourt ronde
- fruits
(St olivière le 12)
- fromages
- Vin

groceries in giverny

Divine Intervention

how lucky she was,
to *be* in the right place
at the right time.

tired and worn down,
her wings had failed to flutter
any longer

then,
divine intervention

like the hands of god,
she was picked up
from the ground
and cradled, ever so gently
by two traveling poets passing by—
they gazed upon her with deep admiration
completely in awe of her, just as she was

they cared for her in her darkest hour,
holding her with softened grasps
until she was strong enough
to fly on her own
once again

sometimes, all we need
is for someone to notice us,
meet us where we are,
and care enough to lift us up;

to just hold us for a little while~

Homesick
(for a place i once thought i was sick of)

i longed for the day when i would leave behind the place i'd
always been- a home that grew to feel more like a prison.
i have always been filled with intense wanderlust; constantly
daydreaming of faraway places... my soul always longed for the
world- like a songbird in a cage.

the time came, and my stomach was full of butterflies,
uncertainty... and grief. i did not expect my first international
adventure to coincide with one of the darkest chapters of my
life. i did not believe that i was strong enough to fly on my
own, so far away- having just lost one of my closest friends
just fifty-four days prior. my world had quite literally flipped
upside down... nevertheless, the wanderlust persisted somewhere
inside of me, buried deep beneath my sorrow. so, off i flew,
within a gust of wind on two white wings- with nothing to lose,
and everything to gain.

when the clouds cleared and my feet touched new soil, i found myself
existing within an overwhelming range of emotions. blissfully
fluttering on french winds, i felt free. but by nightfall,
the darkness had caught up with me, despite the distance i had
traveled to escape it. my mind began silently spiraling inside
of my skull, as my heavy eyes searched frantically for a sign-
one that i could understand. in a sleep-deprived daze, i found
myself stumbling back to the hotel, where i then attempted to
rest my head... but the silence in my room became deafening. i
flipped through the channels on the television, hearing only the
soft mumbles of what seemed like gibberish to my untrained ears.
i was alone, over five thousand miles from home, feeling much
like a child again; in awe of this new world, while equally as
vulnerable. i quickly learned to tuck my fear into this foreign
bed beside me, and surrender.

the next morning, i awoke feeling refreshed and ready to explore
this new place. like a duckling following the row, i carefully
trekked through parisian streets with our group of starlight

SUNSHINE ALEXANDRIA

poets. i soaked up the french culture in total presence-
completely immersed in this new world- though i could still feel
the darkness looming nearby... i began to perceive my life back
home in a whole new way; as home. but when i am there, i crave
to be anywhere but. through such immense heartache, i naturally
craved the familiar to soothe me. but to take off my rose colored
glasses for once: there wasn't much at home to go back to.
like a hermit crab, i had long outgrown my shell- yet now,
outside of that shell, naked and fragile,
i found myself longing for the comfort of it...

maybe home is where you are from, or maybe it changes with you
as you grow. perhaps i will always be in search of my new shell~
a physical place of belonging... with so many places on this
earth which i have not yet touched. i understand now that the
most important home you will ever have is the sanctuary you build
within yourself. i think home is a feeling which i will always
strive to cultivate, no matter where i am. oregon will always be
my first home; it was where i was created, where i took my first
breath, and where i lived my entire life thus far; every past
version of me lives there. the oregon soil has held me through
every period of darkness and every moment of light... throughout
my many lifetimes in this one life.

i realized that oregon, the people i've known and everything
i've been through has shaped me into everything i am-
and without it all, i may not have had the chance to pursue
this dream or explore this new world. a moment of awareness...
understanding that everything which has ever happened to me has
led me to this very moment.

i have learned that travel is both magical and flawed, and i am
embracing it all with gratitude-
knowing someday soon, i will have to return to my first home...
and i will do so with a new pair of eyes, a soul that has been
revitalized,
and a newfound perspective of appreciation for the very place
that i've desired for so long, to escape.

in the city of light
filled with darkness

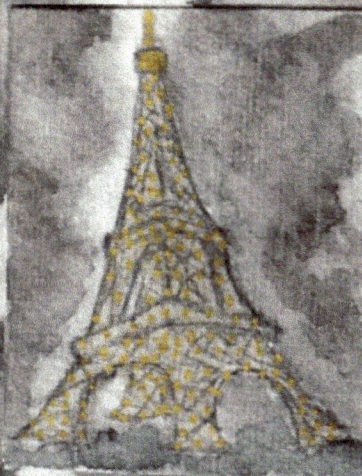

Aiden

i remember
lying on our backs
in the middle of the street
stuck together, earthbound
spinning, faster
gazing at the stars
speaking of existence
and the absence of gravity

glued like magnets
with our backs against the earth
forgetting our anger
and sadness
for a brief moment
in time

i was not prepared
for you to let go;
floating
into the ether
without me—

a rope tied
around your neck,
i tried to unravel it
but it slipped through my fingers;
you were already gone

leaving me behind
to stare at these stars;
pondering the afterlife
without hearing
a response

// *you were always dancing with death*

Hunter

he was childlike,
an innocent soul, so pure
you could see it through his eyes
when they gazed at you~
they were very much alive,
but he was slowly fading, deep inside
and he knew just how to hide

hiding his own pain, underneath a smile~
his heart was bigger than his shadow;
i think giving others the love he needed
soothed his own inner turmoil

when i first met him,
he was just a caterpillar
beautiful, lively & new,
yearning for more

over time,
i watched him slowly transform
until he grew the very wings
he'd always longed for~

but just as he began to flutter,

his heart stopped
spiracles released

he
fell
to
the
earth;

later i learned,
butterflies
never fly
for long

Sunshine Alexandria

Jeana Marie

when i pick up my paintbrush,
i see her in my mind-
every part of her still lives there
and she grins, like the cheshire cat
mischievous & mad
but she looked more like alice

she had long blonde hair & eyes like the sky
and as i paint, so many memories of her flash me by~
i can still see how her baby blues shine
as she paints black eyeshadow
on the lids of her eyes
in the reflection
of her bedroom mirror.

we were just teenagers then,
and she was a couple years older-
like the big sister i always wanted...

she was fearless & passionate,
with a soul wild with wanderlust
and a heart made of fire~
and we fought like sisters, too.

i remember our hands clasped tight
as we took off on our very first flight
& when we landed, we made a pact that night
to see the rest of the world
side by side.

our friendship felt like a movie
but really, she was the star
more like a supernova
just too bright for this world

she burned out fast and suddenly
but her light still illuminates my memories;

SUNSHINE ALEXANDRIA

her laughter still echoes in my mind
and throughout all space & time

she sparkled like no other;
an artist, dancer, singer, lover-
she was the happiest
dancing with fire,
digging in dirt,
or covered in paint.

she was the artist, and now the muse
and she dances all around me
beaming
with each brush stroke

Kindness

she doesn't know
how her kindness
soothes my broken heart;

dark nights in paris
chasing the eiffel tower,
we barely know each other–
yet there is something so familiar
and i do not believe people meet
by accident

she doesn't know
how her presence
makes me feel less alone
like a light in the darkness

i left a lock for you on the bridge
as we watched the iron lady sparkle
for the first time–
you would have loved to see this;
to see the world
and i hope you can see it now–
all of the magic

sleep deprived,
her hand holds mine
at the dinner table
and my heart feels less heavy;
the world, less dark

i am grateful for the kindred souls;
the earthbound angels–
the beacons of light
who guide me through this darkness

and perhaps it is you
from the other side
guiding their gentle hands
to mine

// you always told me i deserved kindness

SUNSHINE ALEXANDRIA

Claude Monet

he spent his life *painting* to leave an impression
unknowingly changing the history for art, forever

they say all artists are somewhat mad,
so i wonder what would keep him up at night
before he drifted off to painted dreamscapes~

he must have been haunted by grief,
losing not one, but *two* wives
and then, his first born child

it is no wonder
he also lost *himself*
in lily ponds and sunflower fields,
living out of paint tubes,
desperately trying to colorize
a world turned gray...

they say monet was not very nice
but you've got to be a bit romantic
to paint the same muse endlessly;
he painted her even in death,
admiring her until her very last breath
but what happens
when the artist's muse dies?

perhaps his pain turned him bitter
but you can't convince me
that artists
aren't just lovers
in disguise

i understand why he threw seeds to soil,
surrounding himself in flowers & greenery~
an abundance of nature
to soothe a broken heart
and harvest endless inspiration

SUNSHINE ALEXANDRIA

SUNSHINE ALEXANDRIA

i lie awake, here in paris, missing you immensely— wishing with all my heart things were different. but it's late, and this hotel room remains dark & empty... commercials on the television speak softly in french, and the light blue hue illuminates the room. i'm thinking of you and... i just hope you are happy. i wish you were here to experience this place with me, i know you would love every moment of it. and anyway, i hope this reaches you soon— i'm not sure how great the postal service is in heaven

à ceux que j'ai

hâte de revoir

111 rue du

Paradis

eternally, Sunshine ♂ ♡

The Artist's Garden in Argenteuil (A Corner of the Garden with Dahlias), 1873 (oil on canvas) by Monet, Claude (1840-1926)

She gave
her whole soul
to one
who never cared
to love her
in the first place...

—s.a.   psyche + cupid

Rebirth

Vernon > Rouen

i caught my reflection in the train window
and i noticed a child staring back at me~
her energy was wild and free
her eyes, a golden green
olive tones, like two serpentine stones
with a dark outer iris of evergreen trees...

she was full of life;
thrown into this new world
with nowhere to be, and everything to discover~
she follows her feet wherever they wander,
fully immersed in the divine flow...
her pure soul *shines* through the windows of her eyes,
not yet haunted by any darkness in her life

the train departed & time sped up
as countryside landscapes blurred together~
i closely watched as the little girl grew older,
everything but her bright eyes changing;
it was then that i realized,
her eyes, were in fact,
mine

my inner child is *beaming*
and oh, how i have missed her~
it has been *so* long
since i've seen my eyes sparkle with wonder~
since i've felt my heart center
burst open with bliss

to travel the world
is to live in alignment with my purpose~
and in this moment, i feel no suffering

i breathe in presence and gratitude
as tears of joy stream down my face
and i let out a cry
much like an infant~

through experiencing the world
i have been reborn

Sunshine Alexandria

je suis né de nouveau

Paris Montmartre

the key

to happiness

is to experience

the world

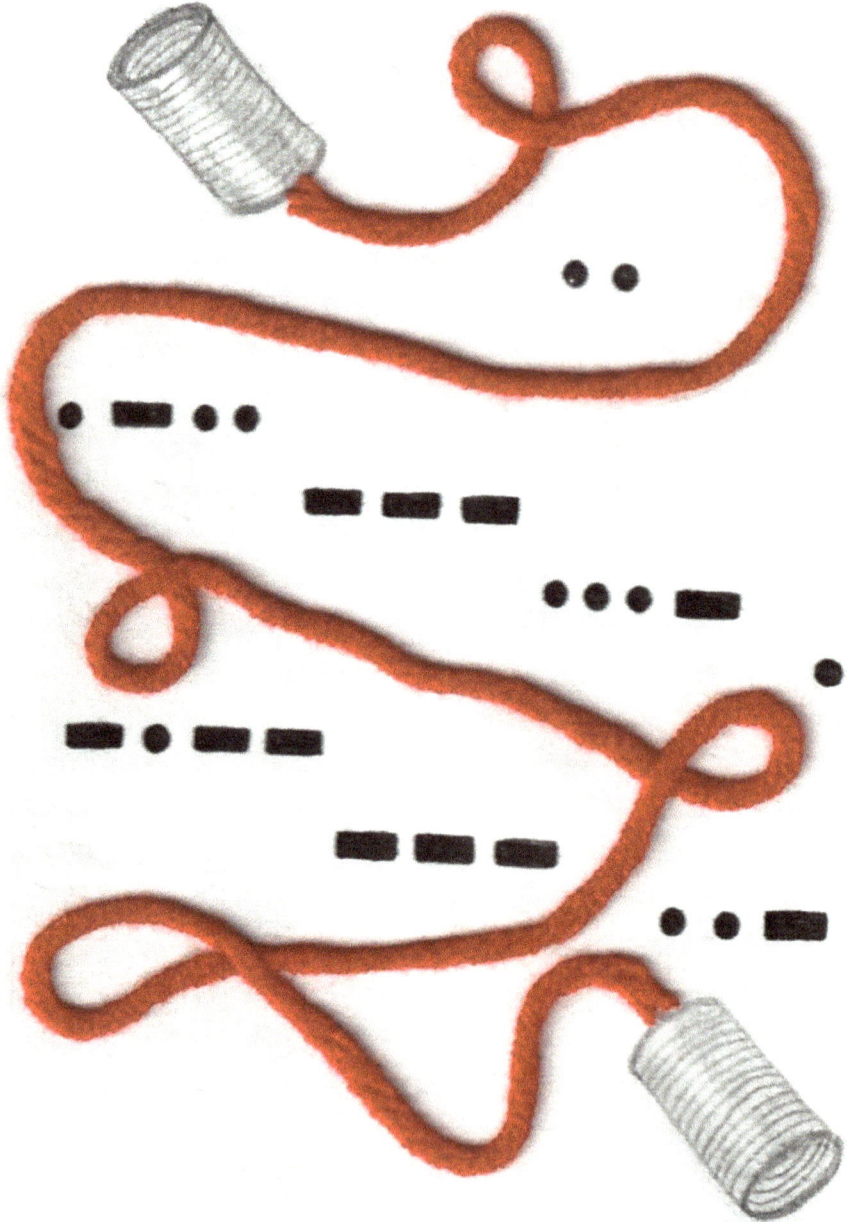

SUNSHINE ALEXANDRIA

Red String

i know you heard it in my voice—
an energy so tangible, yet just out of our grasp.
the gentle cadence wrapping around each word
that we spoke to each other;
it was obvious, and everyone could hear it, see it, feel it
but between you & i, it went unsaid.

our love, an inaudible conversation
between our tethered hearts—
our love, like the red string between two cans,
but neither of us used the right words.

(the truth)
weaving, like twine dancing around our nervous bodies
and the way you understood the threads like muscle memory:
hands weaving stitch patterns

the way you heard it— the frequency of my voice—
not what i said, but *how* i said it—
and in that moment, you looked over at me,
our eyes sharing something
our tongues could not—
my voice like that of morse code:
revealing the hidden messages of my soul
that my ego was too afraid to speak.

when our eyes met that night,
i knew you understood.
and we didn't need to state
with words
what we had already declared
with our irises

Reincarnation

i lay quietly in the garden
overflowing
with gratitude & grief.
weeping *(begging, pleading)*
wishing i could give you my eyes
so you could see
how truly beautiful life could be~
wanting *(needing)* to open up your ribcage
and give you my b e a t i n g heart;
so you could have one more chance...
you deserved to experience bliss,
like this

can you see it, now?
through this lens of mine-
can you see this, *through my mind?*
or maybe you're looking down
from a bird's eye...

a butterfly lands
on my hand,
my journal,
my pen-
and i can't help but wonder
if you've been here all along

fluttering your wings
to the beat of my heart,
crawling around
in the puddles of tears
on the palm of my hand,
whispering these very words
into ink,

is that you?

SUNSHINE ALEXANDRIA

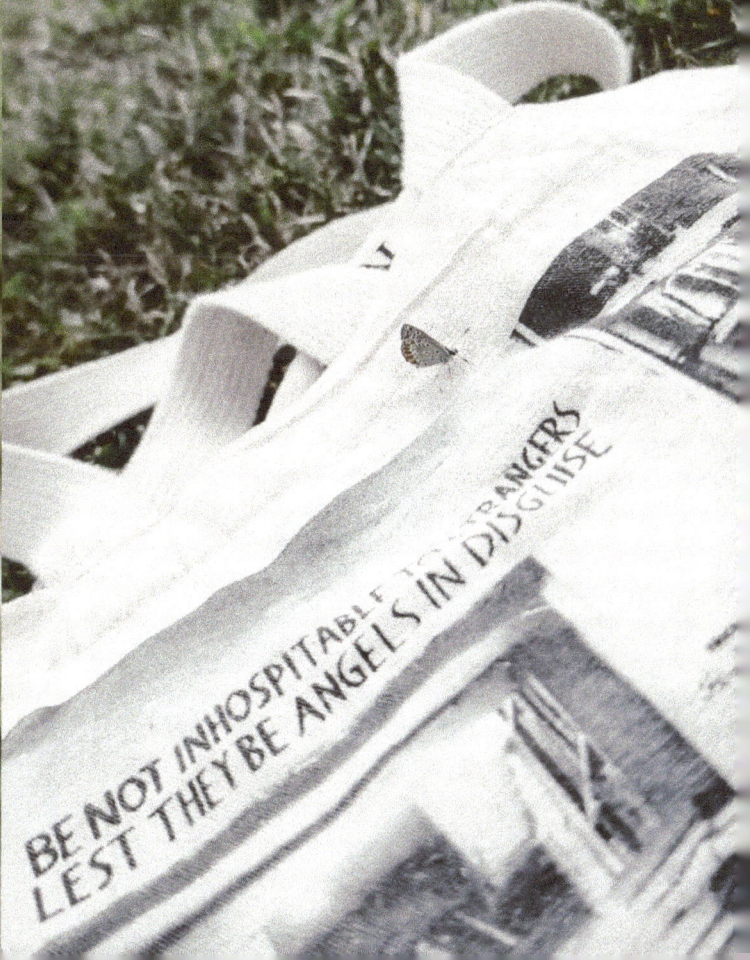

BE NOT INHOSPITABLE TO STRANGERS
LEST THEY BE ANGELS IN DISGUISE

Sharp Memories

i had planned to go somewhere far away,
so i packed memories of you in my suitcase
and i carry them with me everyday
but they keep falling out of my pockets
and when i try to pick them up,
the edges cut me open.

our memories are hard to hold-
like shattered pieces of broken glass
once making up something whole;
i keep trying to put the pieces together,
but i only end up with more blood on my hands.

so...
i tuck them away
back into the deepest parts of my luggage-
somewhere they cannot hurt me, *for now*
but i know some days,
i will have to unpack it all:
bleed it
scream it
cry it out
and allow myself to release
the pain of your absence.

maybe, one day,
the edges will have worn down
and become softer
so i can finally think about you
and smile

instead of die

in my bag

Sheets of Music

i can't seem to throw ink on paper fast enough...
i feel a sense of urgency to write it all down- every detail,
all the magic~ before it one day disappears. before the
flowers die and the photos warp, before my memories fade.
i don't want to forget a single thing about this wondrous
place...

i want to remember
how different the energy feels on this side of the world~
how car horns and foreign chatter fill these old historic
streets,
how the birds fly together and sing,
like a soaring symphony
creating sheets of music in the air~

i want to remember
the sound of cathedral bells ringing all around me~
how romantic street art hides in plain sight;
like handwritten love letters on display for all to read~
how the breeze breathes life into me
and my pashmina dances around my body,
protecting my vulnerable heart.

i want to remember
how the wind whispers sweetly to me
and cobblestone streets guide my nose & my feet
to the smell of fresh *pain au chocolat* down the street
wafting down from a local boulangerie~

i want to remember
france at golden hour~
how sun rays beam down to cleanse the earth
drenching everything in pure, golden light,
before the sky fades to darkness~
then, the iron lady; she comes to life
leaving everyone enamored by her beauty.

in this city of love, i wonder
how many lovers fell for each other
in this exact spot that i am standing~
or how many knees knelt down
with their heads in their hands
and their hearts on the ground...

SUNSHINE ALEXANDRIA

all i know is this; life is full of pain & bliss~
and we must soak it all in *with presence,*
knowing that *all* things
must someday
come to an end.

the beauty of life

scan to hear
the music

SUNSHINE ALEXANDRIA

eleven strangers filled with starlight
from all different parts of the world
became strung together in the evening sky
by one constellation poet~

like shooting stars,
we flew above oceans
and distant, foreign lands
spilling stardust from our souls
to form this creation in your hands.
we navigated unknown territories
and held each other as we explored,
and one would not stop to wonder
if we've done this once before...

so as we share our final poems,
take a rose and close our journals,
i know this is not a goodbye~
for we will always be connected
as one bright cluster in the sky

in a chain of light unbroken
no matter where we are,
i know we'll all be twinkling together
forever, near or far

au revoir,
starlight family

starlight memories

miles of thousands
   away from home
and wandering
   in this place unknown,
your name follows me
   close behind
like telling me
   you're still alive...

.the angel nearby.

~ s.a.

to all of the people

who buried me

deep underground,

(isolating me)
in darkness & dirt;

you pushed me
so
far
beneath
the soil

you hoped
i would never
see sunlight again

and for a while, i didn't;

you were unaware
i was a seed...

and like nature,
i too, am resilient

so i stayed
where you planted me-

each time you pushed me,
i burrowed deeper

until one day

i popped up

on the other side of the world

and bloomed

again

s.a.

SUNSHINE ALEXANDRIA

231

"the one"

i stumbled upon
                    a bevy of swans
two by two
                    each pair floats along
        all, except one.
one swan
            swimming in circles
                    seeming ever so lost-
a silent longing
fills the air around her;
a soft sadness drips d
                      o
                      w
                      n

from her eyes
to her feathers-

she swims
in a lake
of her own tears

                    sunshine alexandria
                        s.a.

47

7 P 1/250 F 11 +0.7 E

5

venus de milo

could it be?
the goddess of love...
frozen in marble

without limbs to embrace her lover,
she longs to hold, and be held
but she is eternally misunderstood...

only *she* knows
all that she has been through
and with lips sealed shut,
she can not tell.

she stands still
throughout time—
centuries passing,
waiting for
the one;

the one to study
all of her curves
and cracks,
gazing deeply enough
to read the true story
beneath her skin

she's weathered- imperfect,
yet *beautiful*
from every angle,
despite her slow decay

she holds out *hope*
that one will truly see her
for all that she is,
and decide to accept her
with the same unconditional love
that she gives

SUNSHINE ALEXANDRIA

Wall of Love

je t'aime
te quiero
ich liebe dich

i could tell you
i love you
in every language,

but you
do not understand
the dialect

of my heart

Volim te
Saya cinta padamu
I love you
KOCHAM CIĘ
rad te imam
Mo férân re

I ♥ PARIS

i have
a thirst
for faraway places;

a need
to dig my toes
into untouched soil–

i dream
of exploring other worlds:
with a pollen covered nose
& an exercised tongue,

i want
to inhale foreign flowers
and forget the sound
of my own language

wanderlust

SUNSHINE ALEXANDRIA

Grief

7.31.2023

i'd be lying if i said the **grief** didn't follow me onto the plane,
like an uninvited guest taking up too much space within this home
that is my body. it hovers over me- whether engulfing my entire
being, or gently looming in the background- it is a persistent
darkness which never rests. i'm still trying to figure out how
to accept that this will always be a part of me, and learning
to embrace the moments when it seems to consume every ounce of
hope that i have left. somewhere inside of me, i believe that the
light must eventually return... *it will, right?* i am terrified
of feeling this way forever. grief is agonizing, but i have
learned that we must move through it, letting it flow through
and out of us like water- trusting that we won't be drowning in
it forever; knowing *feeling* is the only way to come back up for
air.

if life were a painting, grief would be like paint thinner-
suddenly poured all over the canvas, watering everything down
until we forget what it looked like before-
lost in a blurry world. in order to create a colorful life again,
we have to use new paint and try different techniques.

if you are no stranger to grief, you know that a piece of you dies
along with the people you lose. you must reach deep to find the
strength to bring yourself back to life- in order to survive.
grief teaches us how to care for ourselves; to turn inward and
embrace change. the uncomfortable truth is, after loss, you can
not stay the same. when death brushes so near, you have to find
new ways of living. it is essential to seek experiences that make
you feel alive again. partake in things you usually wouldn't;
things that deeply soothe you and set your soul on fire.

drive to a viewpoint and scream until your pain echoes throughout
other worlds. stand barefoot in the rain and let it cleanse
your broken heart. lay in the grass and breathe with the earth-
noticing the butterflies, birds and bees all around you. take a
drive without a destination, book a train or a flight, or just
take a walk somewhere you've never been and let your spirit
freely wander. let your heart guide you to the experiences that
you are called to. adventure has always been at the core of my
heart, and it has always shown me the beauty again, even in my
darkest moments. grief will try and make you a prisoner of your
own mind; just know that you are in control. get out into the

world and let new experiences resuscitate your soul. trying new things and spending time in nature will show you the magic again. you must allow yourself to go searching for your joy; your reasons to live. and it doesn't need to be far- you can find magic in your own backyard. remember that our physical time here is finite- and to be alive right now is a privilege many do not live to experience. i promise, you will find joy again. it may come in small doses, but it will come- and you must allow yourself first, to go searching for it.

we all carry fragments of the people we've lost, and it's our mission to live on, in all of the ways that they can't. living our lives to the fullest is how we honor ourselves and the dead. you owe it to yourself to live like your life depends on it, because it does. it's okay to allow the pain of grief to wash over you when it comes, like the waves of an ocean- but try not to stay there for too long- let it hurt until your salty tears have dried and released some of that heaviness, then, after the waves have crashed into you and you feel even a brief moment of calm, remember to nurture yourself... i can not say that the ocean of grief will always be calm, but you are powerful enough to survive the storms.

if you take anything from loss, understand that life and time are precious, and love is all that matters. learn to live and love right now. take the leap, follow your dreams, get your passport, book the flight, write the words, create the thing. you *must* chase after joy and create the happiness you seek, while you still can. even when grief clings onto you like a shadow- it is better to have your toes deep in the sand and the sun kissing your cheek while you weep. this human experience is too special to become a living ghost- to be stuck inside your past, your mind, four walls, one city, one state, one country... get out there and let the magic of the entire world hold your weeping soul- let the earth carry you as you dig up parts of yourself that were buried, or you never knew existed. there is no limit to how beautiful life can truly be when you choose to listen to the whispers of your soul. no matter how dark life has become, i promise you: there is always the chance to find more light.

let mother nature heal our broken hearts, and may the wonders of the world lead us all back home to ourselves.

SUNSHINE ALEXANDRIA

Photographay by
Sunshine Alexandria

I taught our final Art & Poetry workshop in the garden beneath Reims Cathedral— where French kings were historically crowned!

Art & Poetry Workshop 3

Topics:
— Poetry as a way of life
— Divine, Internal, & External Inspiration
— The search for significance

"The inspiration is the best part of the poem and you had nothing to do with it." "You see the world for the first time as a child, the rest is just a memory." "Poetry is the highest class of writing. The product is better than those that produce it." "You see the beauty in something when you know it will change. It will fade. It will die." — Arthur Smith, 1948–2018

     Poet— please— don't let the beauty die.

Prompt 1: There are 372 statues in the garden of Versailles. Find the one that speaks out to you. Write a poem to the statue OR in the voice of that statue.

Prompt 2: Write a poem with the title "The Secrets of Versailles" and describe little details that likely go unnoticed or are ignored by others.

Prompt 3: Write a poem incorporating the phrase, "By the light of the sun,
     do not let me forget..."

We wandered through Reims Cathedral, the air thick with centuries of prayer and devotion...

By the Seine, dancers swayed like willows in the wind, their elegance mirroring the river's quiet pulse

Vanessa

keep off grass says the
Sign at the edge of green
But not for the ravens
who are the gardeners
for the king

VANESSA WILSON

Protector of Reims

VANESSA WILSON

Navigator

Fierce angel-
I'd trust your direction
straight from the start.
For even though you've
lost your eyes,
I'll always follow your heart.

Navigator

"POOR DENIS"   07.10.23 MW

La Nuit

You may be the night
but you're never in darkness,
for if you keep your desire,
you'll never lose your fire.

La Nuit

SQUARE JEHAN RICTUS - PARIS   07.05.23   MW

IN FRANCE   07.05.23

TOUR EIFFEL   07.10.23   MW

VANESSA WILSON

Trois Grâces

VANESSA WILSON

Trust

Take this which I let you hold.
Be gentle,
for you will find that she is finite
and should be treated with kindness
 as if every day,
may be her last.

As fragile as this butterfly,
So is this heart.

Both I trust you with.

Trust

A Moment in Time

VANESSA WILSON

Champagne Lounge

Always Home

Remember this moment-

so far away from the home you knew as a child
the home you grew up in.
Learned right from wrong
watched patience and empathy practiced to perfection.
Even further from the home you made
With humans who went from strangers
to friends
to family.

In this moment
alone on the grass
beneath walls perhaps older than even your country
surrounded by flowers that remind you of childhood.

By the light of the sun,
do not let me forget-
even here, even now, on this earth

I am home.

Stolen

Stolen

I long for the farm of which I onced called home.
I wish to reach out for it
but like my freedom
my arms are also gone.
Faces come and go
and while i'd like to go with them
to see the sky outside
the green grass
feel the breath of air against my smooth skin
I cannot.
Instead I stand-
unable to pull up my fabric
unable to look away from the cold stone that
surrounds me.
Unable to go home.

VANESSA WILSON

Forbidden Flight

Hold tight, I say,
don't let go or be scared.
It's a long journey, I know,
But drop you,
I'd never.

Take flight, she whispers,
for I cannot go with you.
Remember our love,
and together, I promise,
we'll be forever.

Forbidden Flight

Photographay by
Vanessa Wilson

Caught at a crossroads— the Sunflowers turn
their bright faces away from the Sky to show me which
way to go and I carry my darkness all the way to the city of light

To be transformed
To be forged anew
To begin again KS
To travel new places
and get lost in time
never forgetting the incredible journey
never letting the memories we cherish
slip away or fade into oblivion—
~~and~~ how can a heart hold a moment in time?

How can I hold you in my arms
when you're just as fleeting?
I suppose I'll have to remain a favorite chapter.
Even though my book was never born from beauty
I wrote it in blood so my words would bare the J.S.
    with
weight of this burdened body in a world without you
Each step is a toll on the warning bell that is my heart
There is no melody, no song to listen for if
The score I keep now, is only notes of you

Notes made up of syllables, words tasting both sweet & tart
Made of A flats and D minors, singing the tone of your
voice, and your heart - I'm captivated LoA.

Our arms entwined, we lay like silverware
My fingers caught in tousled hair
Two clocks ticking out of sync   MR
Wishing our hands would align again
    even if for just a moment   S.t.
I know our hearts will always beat as one
As dependable as the twinkling lights
as cherished as the memories & history
Together, in this lifetime   MW
                    and the next

Lauren Craft
Freydis Ivar
Holly Dow Room
        Sunshine Alexandria

Emma Mitchell

Rachel Clyfe
Kendall Gordon
Karsich Fish
May-Anne Raven
Vanessa Wilson

Bonjour lovelies ♡ ♡ ✴✴
I hope this finds you well...
Today was like magic...
Vernon, France... but today I took a bike to
Giverny and visited Monet's
garden. It was breathtaking.
On the way there, I was
greeted by cows, horses,
goats, and sunflower fields.
I thought of you both as i
rode my bike in the warm summer wind, past
fields of yellow as far as the eyes could see ♡
Thank you for inspiring me and opening up my
world to the gift of international travel!
Love, Sunshine ✴

RACHEL & LAURA CLIFT

TENNESSEE
USA

Fondation Claude Monet
GIVERNY
www.claude-monet...
Tél. 02 32 51 28 21

Claude Monet (1840-1926) devant sa maison à Giverny
© Photo : Musée d'Orsay, Dist. RMN-Grand Palais / Patrice Schmidt
EDITIONS D'ART JACK · 22700 LOUANNEC
RÉF. : 12958

253 16

FRANCE
international

You guide me like a star

I am only a wanderer and
you guide me like a star-

Emma, the one that captures those
around her and proclaims them as art.
You guide me like a star-
Freydis, the one who loves
with every breath and brushstroke.
You guide me like a star-
J.S., the one on a never-ending journey,
ever searching, ever seeking.
You guide me like a star-
Kassidy, the one whose laughter is enough
to make our sorrows & fears fade away.
You guide me like a star-
Kendall, the one who has always been a poet, and
always will be, whether she believes it (yet) or not.
You guide me like a star-
Leisly, the one made of moonbeams and kindness
to spare, inspiring and enchanting as the night sky.
You guide me like a star-
Mary-Anne, the one who has rekindled the flame of
poetry in her heart, and burns brighter than ever.
You guide me like a star-
Sunshine, the one whose presence or absence is felt-
like the moon- every phase of her cherished equally.
You guide me like a star-
Vanessa, the one that holds any lonely hand and fills
me with courage- a muse, a poet, a sister.

I am only a wanderer and
you guide me like a star,
thank you for lighting the way.

Ever yours,
xx R.

Find us beyond the page

Emma Riddoch
IG: @EMC2_77

Freydis Lova
IG: @FREYDIS.LOVA

FREYDISLOVAPOETRY.COM

J.S.
IG: @HEARTLESSNOMADPOETRY

Kassidy Fisk
IG: @KASS_FISK5

Kendall Josten
IG: KENDALL.BOOKS

Leisly Roman
IG: @_LITERARYHOPE

Mary-Anne Ramirez
IG: @MARYANNEBYDESIGN

Sunshine Widmer
IG: @S.A.POETESS

Vanessa Wilson
IG: @NESSERS77

L. A. Clift
IG: @L.A.CLIFT

LAURACLIFT.COM

R. Clift
IG: @R.CLIFTPOETRY

RCLIFTPOETRY.COM

Scan for links to poetry books written by my Starlight Poets!

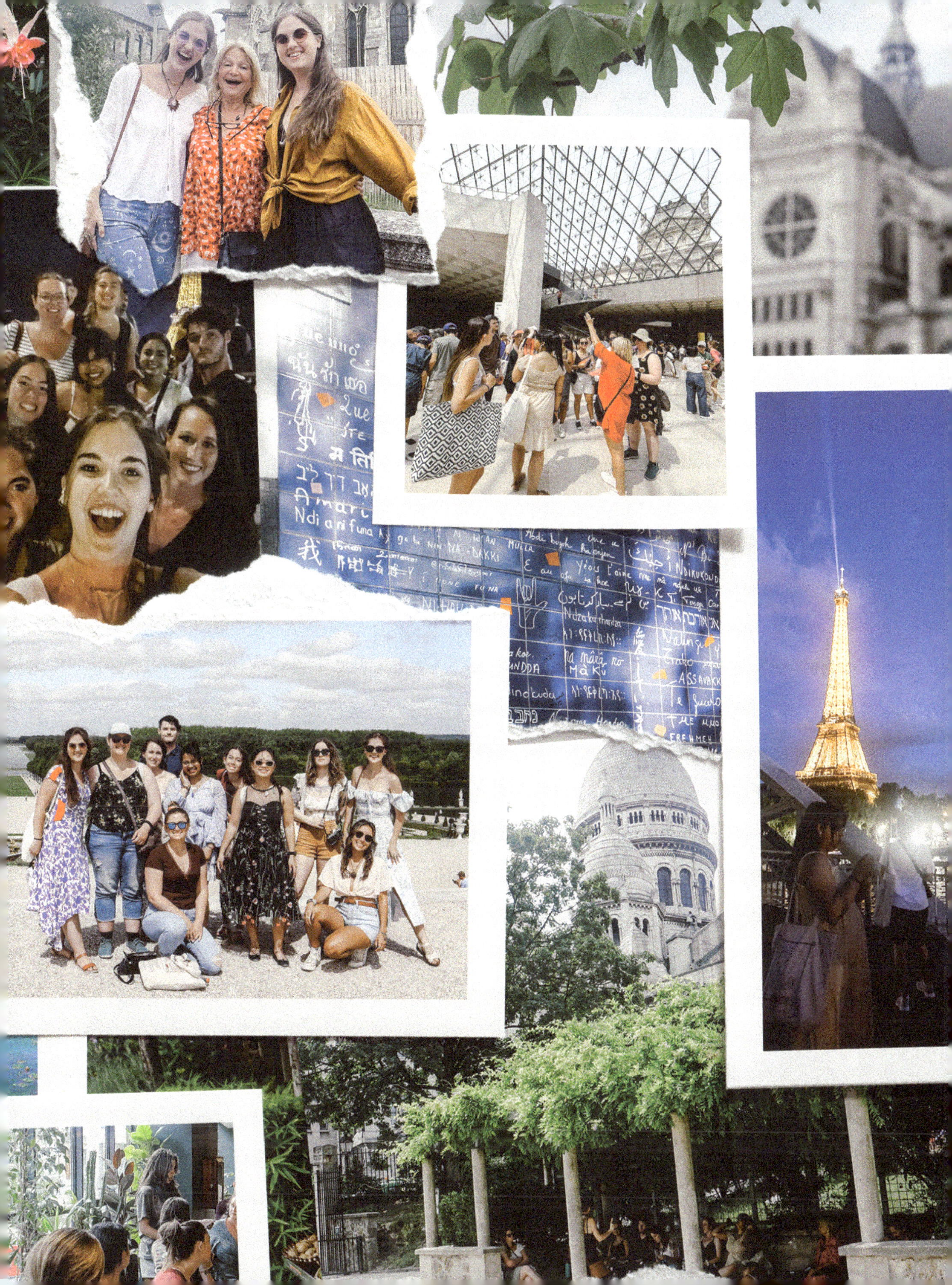

DIGITAL ARCHIVE OF PHOTOS, VIDEOS, & MORE

ISBN: 978-1-960045-06-5 (paperback),
978-1-960045-09-6 (hardback).

Book design & layout by Rachel Clift.
Cover design by Rachel Clift.
rcliftpoetry.com

First printing edition, 2024.

Travel Itinerary organized and operated by
TrovaTrip.
trovatrip.com

Milton Keynes UK
Ingram Content Group UK Ltd.
UKHW051003061224
452242UK00018B/187

9 781960 045065